Service-Learning

Service-Learning

What Every ESL Teacher Needs to Know

by

Trisha Dowling and James M. Perren

University of Michigan Press
Ann Arbor

First paperback edition 2023
Copyright © Trisha Dowling and James M. Perren, 2021
All rights reserved
Published in the United States of America by the
University of Michigan Press

Paperback ISBN: 978-0-472-03949-4
Ebook ISBN: 978-0-472-12734-4

First published September 2021

CONTENTS

Introduction: Purpose and Scope

Service-Learning: What Every ESL Teacher Needs to Know responds to the growth of TESOL service-learning (TSL). This publication adds to the applied linguistics and teacher resource literature base with best practices in TSL and teaching English as a second/foreign language (ESL/EFL). We use the term "TESOL service-learning" and the acronym "TSL" introduced by Barbara Cooney repeatedly in this ebook (Cooney, 2015). The increase in the TSL literature suggests interest and demand for foundational knowledge that will help guide teacher practice (Fitzgerald, 2009; Kincaid & Sotiriou, 2004; Perren & Wurr, 2015; Wurr, 2013). Nevertheless, none of the existing and relevant TSL publications provide short, easy-to-use explanations for materials, nor descriptions for how to start using TSL as an ESL teacher (or as an EFL teacher) from a practical orientation.

Clear information on how to coordinate the proper strategies for implementation of service-learning in TESOL are available and located at various institutions. But there is a need for practical information about how to carry out service-learning pedagogy as well as how to maintain critical community partnerships. This publication offers practical answers regarding what ESL teachers need to know about service-learning. We also show possibilities for teaching beginning-level ESL students in the community with online service-learning opportunities, as this is needed in today's context of virtual learning.

What Is TESOL Service-Learning?

Key Terms and Definitions

In defining **service-learning**, the earliest definition we found is "the accomplishment of tasks that meet genuine human needs in combination with conscious educational growth," originating from the Southern Regional Education Board in the late 1960s (Stanton et al., 1999, p. 2). However, service-learning has also progressed into "a pedagogy integrating student learning and student reflection while serving in communities as partners with community organizations" (Eyler & Giles, 1999). As traditional service-learning scholars (which we distinguish from those writing from the field of TESOL), Eyler and Giles (1999) imply a "curricular" aspect with a connection to the main academic content, which in ESL would likely be a language-related area such as the traditional four skills, grammar, and vocabulary. More information about the ESL content will be presented in Chapter 2, "Strategies for Successful Community Partnerships."

A second key term used is **experiential learning**, which is traced to John Dewey and two principles he proposed for the philosophy of experience: the Principle of Continuity and the Principle of Interaction (Dewey, 1938). Experiential learning is an important term for ESL teachers because of the emphasis in TSL of learning out of the classroom, specifically in the community. The experience of being outside of the four walls of the traditional classroom allows for direct application of English as a second language content in authentic, real-world settings.

Another key term used in TSL is **community partner (CP)**, which is a noun reflecting both a partner (as in the dictionary definition sense) and a concept that relates to the reciprocity element of general service-learning (Furco, 1996). An important aspect of CP development includes TESOL educators utilizing service-learning by "acknowledging and accepting the professional contributions of community partners as co-educators" (Wurr & Perren, 2015, p. 11). The concept of shared responsibility between recipient of the service and beneficiary of the learning has been an emerging notion during the historical growth of service-learning (Stanton et al., 1999). Researchers have highlighted the significance of CP's role in service-learning in TSL literature (Schneider, 2019; Wendler Shah, 2015; Wurr & Perren, 2015).

Social justice is a relevant term to TESOL service-learning and provides ESL teachers with additional knowledge about how service-learning pedagogy compliments social movements. Social justice is "the way in which human rights are manifested in the everyday lives of people at every level of society" (Edmund Rice Centre, 2000, as cited in Hemphill, 2015, p. 4). The term and concept are not new to English as a second language education (Hafernik et al., 2002). Conceptualizing social justice in our field has directed attention to ethical dilemmas and issues ESL faculty may experience. This earlier publication defined the corollary concept, **ethics**, as the responsibilities and obligations we have to students, faculty colleagues, and society, both inside and outside the classroom; this is one reason why social justice is applicable. Many practical activities were outlined within the pages of this early social justice/ethics resource material. It was followed shortly after by another highly practical publication (Messerschmitt & Hafernik, 2009). More recently, social justice has been traced to TSL and its connection to pedagogical practices and research centered on IEP students as research participants make a transition in their post-service stage from simply an awareness level to critical consciousness and then longer-term continued action (Cameron, 2015).

Finally, the term **reflection** represents the formal learning process. In service-learning, reflection is considered a high-impact educational practice; students have to both "apply what they are learning in real-world settings and *reflect* in a classroom setting on their service experiences" (Kuh, 2008, p. 11, emphasis added). Reflection is an important topic in service-learning and has been written about extensively in general service-learning as well as in TSL. These foundational terms and definitions facilitate a more complete understanding of the information presented in this ebook.

Service-learning is a teaching and learning strategy/pedagogy that teaches civic responsibility, strengthens communities, and integrates meaningful community service with instruction and reflection to enrich learning (National Service-Learning Clearinghouse, 2011). Furthermore, service-learning is accomplished when both the recipients of volunteer service and the providers benefit from the activities (Sigmon, 1979). This ebook aims to assist educators in the planning and use of relevant materials, activities, and assessment in their ESL service-learning classes. It encompasses how to effectively utilize the reflective processes as a focus of student language development through service-learning.

Scope

Information about how TESOL educators can initiate TSL projects in course expansions is presented in Chapter 1, "Service-Learning—Where Do I Begin?" Also discussed in this section is how to sell service-learning to the administration (and to your students). Initiating and maintaining mutually beneficial community partnerships is discussed in Chapter 2, "Strategies for Successful Community Partnerships." Then information about how to integrate relevant TESOL content areas in TSL, providing TESOL educators with a variety of options for breadth and depth of a particular pedagogical concept in a specific educational setting (see also Kumaravadivelu, 2006), is presented in Chapter 3, "I'm Ready....Now What Do I Teach?" The essential concept of reflection as assessment in service-learning is expanded on in Chapter 4, "Assessment in TESOL Service-Learning." We examine how to connect relevant and practical testing measures to key issues in current applied linguistics and service-learning. We also discuss socially situated language-in-use assessment. Thoughts and suggestions based on research and practice (praxis) on how TSL could further evolve and improve is addressed in Chapter 5, "Making It Meaningful." Our interest is to continue the academic conversation about TSL usefulness for any educator in our discipline, whether the context be ESL or EFL. The potential for enhancing TSL with a principle-based understanding of how to align ESL learning objectives with service-learning objectives through a standardization process is discussed. A summary with some final thoughts and suggestions concludes this ebook.

We would also like to point out something about the applicability of the ideas in this publication for different learners and educators. Our combined experiences are primarily with international students working in intensive English programs around the United States. With that stated, most of what we describe relates to how trained ESL teachers with graduate TESOL degrees or teaching certificates can implement these ideas. However, the same materials and concepts can also be used in teacher training programs that include ESL certification programs. Furthermore, because of page number restrictions in this publication, we provide only introductory information on a number of related topics. The interested reader can easily find information through cursory key-word searches on the internet related to K–12 education (Ediger, 2014), adult education, and higher education. Appendix C includes various types of service-learning resources. We have also integrated several learning activities throughout this ebook referred to as "Explorations." These Exploration activities can be matched to the needs of ESL learners in your TSL courses. They are located in final sections of related content and we encourage you to experiment as much as possible and adapt them as needed.

1. Service-Learning—Where Do I Begin?

Let's now consider how service-learning (SL) can be incorporated into different types of courses. In the era of Covid-19, or where remote instruction is all that is possible, this is a serious issue in terms of how to accomplish service learning without in-person interactions, but there are other concerns as well. Although TSL is becoming more widely accepted as beneficial for improving L2 learning and community connections for ESL students, it is not always possible to initiate an entire SL-focused course. In academic content-area courses that include SL (such as engineering, business, or social work), the learning objective focus may be created in a balanced manner, which will include matching one content learning objective with one SL (or social justice) learning objective in each lesson. This type of matching mirrors a best-practice concept outlined in many SL materials (CSU Center for Community Engagement, 2010; Howard, 2001). If we were the rulers of the world, we would suggest maintaining academic rigor in TESOL service-learning (TSL) by establishing a policy (or guideline) of matching one SL objective with one L2 education objective for each lesson or phase of a lesson. Constraints on monetary and human resources in education in general, and specifically in ESL Departments, sometimes means that departments may decide to focus on a more traditional language learning curriculum, which leaves innovation potentially suffering.

The good news is that with a little motivation and planning, existing resources can help you locate ideas and materials for TSL syllabi, lesson plans and activities, and assessment (sites.google.com/site/tesolservicelearning/). First, you should learn about specific models for establishing SL courses and materials (such as the one featured on the Vanderbilt University website [Bandi, 2020]) so you can see how you would like to utilize and adapt your own SL approach in your teaching. Additionally, Perren and Wurr (2015) provide several ideas for incorporating TSL concepts for domestic and international students.

Let's also be clear about one point—integrating SL can be very labor-intensive, especially for an ESL teacher with little information available for how to get started and move forward (Cooney, 2015; Perren, 2013; Perren & Wurr, 2015), which is one of the primary reasons we have written this ebook.

In some cases, one individual has been responsible for the ongoing implementation of SL for an entire region as a result of that person's internal passion and motivation to provide services to a deserving community (Cooney, 2015). Yet there are also powerful and compelling stories of building meaningful and long-lasting connections with organizations and individuals within institutions and the community that integrate service-learning with ESL students (Ene & Orlando, 2015). Examples such as these provide solid evidence that yes, although the workload can be heavy for ESL teachers when integrating SL, as the old saying goes, "Many hands make light work." This reminds us to search for ways to work smarter rather than work harder. As a bit of cautionary advice, what we have found that works in our situations is a significant amount of trial and error by learning how to connect with the appropriate resources and committing ourselves to only as much as we can handle. We suggest that ESL teachers think seriously about the amount of work required before considering any type of out-of-the-classroom SL experience.

Selling Service-Learning to Administration (and to Your Students!)

Perhaps you are fortunate enough to have an administration that is fully on board with the idea of service-learning. TSL research shows how important it is to have a collaborative and coordinated administrative effort to be efficient and effective for students and CPs (Ene & Orlando, 2015). If this is the case, this section may not be for you. Maybe you would like to start a SL class or just add a SL component to your already existing ESL courses. In this case, you may need to provide some justification for those making the curricular decisions. Here are several useful resources and reasons to support your integration of SL.

Reason 1: Greater Autonomy

Service-learning helps ESL students learn more about the community that they live in and advance deeper connections to their community. ESL students of all levels can benefit from increased autonomy. Creating circumstances within the classroom where students can choose the type of community partner (CP) or the type of work that they complete helps generate the autonomy necessary for being a successful student and community member. For instance, Miller and colleagues (2015) reported that students commented overwhelmingly on the sense of agency they gained from SL activities. Also, TSL course instructors have arranged for ESL students to provide volunteer service with an assortment of CPs. As a result, ESL students can have widely varied learning experiences (favorable and unfavorable). It has been reported that implementing multiple CPs in TSL courses can influence comparable learning outcomes (Askildson et al., 2013). Remedies for this challenge are increased preparation for peer facilitators (CPs) and more student supervision by instructors at CP sites that both serve to align "expectations of students and community partners throughout the process" (Askildson et al., 2013, p. 428). Students can also form greater autonomy by having the opportunity to independently reach out and find their own SL situations and service options.

Reason 2: Better Global Citizens

Through SL, student volunteers become more aware of important social issues and themes. However, international students from certain cultures or backgrounds may not be aware of relevant social themes in your teaching context. In some cases, ESL students may not be comfortable discussing these inequalities or social issues although "volunteers learn significantly about topics related to the vision and operational realities of the organizations they are involved with" (Duguid et al., 2013, p. 27). Through SL projects, students make connections to social justice issues and work to "make a difference, not just for individuals in their communities, but also for the larger society" (Wade, 2001, p. 5). By building a better understanding of the vision, focus, and mission statements of organizations, students can expand critical thinking skills that enable them to find solutions to these social problems.

Reason 3: Complex Tasks Improve Linguistic Knowledge

There is extensive research that indicates a relationship between language learning and physical or complex tasks. Schmidt-Kassowa and colleagues (2010), looked at the implications of simultaneous exercise and vocabulary acquisition and found that this enhanced L2 vocabulary learning. Liu and colleagues (2017) recently found that the acquisition of L2 vocabulary is higher when students performed a physical activity versus when they were static. This research supports improved language acquisition through activities such as SL, which requires students to step outside of their comfort zone and learn through complex tasks outside of the classroom. In fact, research has shown statistically significant improvements in English language proficiency in a somewhat abbreviated time period through SL methodology (Askildson et al., 2013). Along with the notion that physical activity can improve linguistic knowledge, the positive relationship between task complexity and learning opportunities indicates that complex tasks can also function as learning vehicles that promote learners' ability to collaborate and construct linguistic knowledge in the process (Kim & Taguchi, 2016). These collaboration and communication skills will serve students well in future courses and in the job market.

Reason 4: Create Meaningful Learning Experiences

Intergenerational SL is commonly used in gerontology and adult development and aging courses to create more meaningful learning experiences (Karasik, 2013; Roodin et al., 2013). Intergenerational SL is meaningful for both students and residents because both groups form connections with people outside of their immediate social circles. As an ESL teacher, you can create meaningful learning experiences by explicitly integrating interactional activities with different types of CP needs that focus on social responsibility. Meaning comes through an alignment of skill-blending because "all available empirical, theoretical, and pedagogical information points to the need to integrate language skills for effective language teaching" (Kumaravadivelu, 2006, p. 206). You can increase your student civic engagement further by structuring detailed readings about social issues that affect their community. In that way, you will also promote a more engaged society. As you coordinate making meaningful learning by integrating skills, you can also include SL activities that relate to many topics such as the environment.

Link Student Learning Outcomes from the Syllabus to Materials

Make your intentions and goals clear to ESL students. Add learning outcomes related to the combination of community engagement and student learning about ESL content to your syllabus; all learning activities done in and out of class should be linked to clear learning objectives. Student learning outcomes can include ideas such as phrases that came from syllabi we previously created in our ESL courses with SL: *increase knowledge of community issues while increasing community interactions; develop an understanding of their own roles and the roles of others in the community.* Activities and resources aligned with these types of learning outcomes can move students closer to achieving the course outcomes.

Readily available resources can play an integral role in the classroom. Teachers can use news articles with a local or national focus to address course themes and practice reading skills. Depending on your students' English language proficiency levels, you can focus on vocabulary from the news articles, ask students to write article summaries, and then discuss or debate these topics in class. By engaging in local news content and relevant information, students are learning about where they live and, eventually, can achieve the outcome of *increasing knowledge of community issues.* Students are then able to deepen the community interactions that they engage in through education in and understanding of local issues (CSUN Community Engagement, 2020).

Another important beginning task is to choose one or two social themes for your ESL class to focus on, such as homelessness, food deserts, incarceration, or race relations. One option is to focus initially on the theme from a local perspective and then ask students to consider the theme from a national or global perspective. You might also consider asking students to vote for the themes they would like to focus on. Though this strategy is more labor intensive as you have less time to prepare beforehand, the benefit of providing students a voice in syllabus construction helps promote their agency (Breen & Littlejohn, 2000). Consequently, they are more likely to be invested in the course and activities.

In concluding this section, we suggest that you pursue resources for guidance within your educational institution or place of employment for more information and training about how to conduct experiential learning activities. Additional resources for virtual teaching of TSL are available in Appendix C. Of particular use for general virtual course development is the California State University/Long Beach (CSULB) website for community engagement (https://www.csulb.edu/center-for-community-engagement).

2. Strategies for Successful Community Partnerships

One of the most potentially overwhelming and time-consuming aspects of setting up a TSL activity or class is finding an appropriate community partnership (CP). This is when you may have to get a little creative and use or even expand your own network to increase your own community engagement, even during a time of remote instruction (as during the Covid-19 pandemic). Begin with an initial search on the Volunteer Match website.

Finding Community Partners

Before making extra work for yourself, do some research around your own campus. SL partnerships are often prevalent in educational settings from K–12 to the university. Many universities now have their own iteration of a department or unit devoted to SL because it has become more common to have some type of service requirement for all undergraduates. For example, at the University of Michigan, the go-to department is called the Ginsberg Center for Student Engagement (https://ginsberg.umich.edu/student-eng agement). If your university has this type of resource, take advantage of it. At your institution's website, you can find community partners that others on campus have previously worked with, pedagogical support and training, and perhaps, even transportation options. At the Ginsberg Center, consultants will guide you through the process of developing an engaged academic learning course. For additional examples of educational institutions with successful ESL programs that regularly use SL, see Ene and Orlando (2015) and Wagner and Lopez (2015). In some cases, staff that are part of a unit devoted to community involvement are tasked with locating, negotiating, and securing volunteer and SL placements for courses and programs; they can gather and share this information for you.

Even if you do not have a department dedicated to community engagement or SL, there may be people around campus who are already doing this type of work. Reach out to like-minded individuals on campus to see what is being done to avoid unnecessary repetition of work. Find out what CPs have worked well (or not well) for student groups. Read the school newspaper or website and find out what student organizations are doing as service. Search for student-created organizations that you could make connections with. If searching takes you nowhere, perhaps send emails to the heads of departments inquiring about existing service projects. Making community connections does not only happen off campus but also on campus.

Transporting Students to the Community Partner Locations

Transportation to CP locations will vary depending on where both your class and the community partner are located, the age of the students, and the structure of the service. Instructors in K–12 obviously have more transportation restrictions than instructors in higher education. Because of the variation of these regulations at the K–12 level, we will not go into extensive detail about transportation for SL. In these cases, instructors should refer to the guidelines already in place at their institutions or in the TSL research as previously reported (Perren, 2013). In higher education, transportation will depend upon several factors. Once again, if your institution has a department focused on setting up service learning/community engagement opportunities, clear guidelines for transportation likely already exist. At the University of Michigan, there is something called *CEAL Ride* in which vehicles are provided for community-based learning courses (lsa.umich.edu/ceal/ceal-ride. html). With a valid driver's license, both students and instructors can go through training and reserve vehicles to transport themselves or small groups. However, this is a rarity in most institutions, so you probably need to make alternative transportation plans.

If public transportation is available in your location, use it. Students may already be familiar with it, and for those who are not, it provides a learning opportunity, a way to become more connected to the community in which they live, and also benefits the environment. In some cases, students may need to drive themselves or their classmates to CP locations. If this is the most logical solution, consider using a *liability waiver*. A quick search of your school name along with liability waiver may lead you to an extensive policy waiving the institution of liability for off-campus excursions. For your particular class, students should also sign an *assumption of risk and release of liability form* (you can find examples of this form online). Consult with your campus SL partners to ensure that proper measures are in place to keep all parties safe in regard to risk management issues during off-campus activities.

Maintaining Positive Relationships with Community Partners

Most integral to the SL experience is maintaining positive relationships with your CPs. If a negative experience occurs, there is not only the potential of harming the reputation of your institution, but also the potential for negative feelings to develop toward international students as a whole or specific populations from certain countries. Wurr and Perren (2015) describe international and generation 1.5 students completing tasks as service providers and encountering "hesitation and awkward interactions" with CPs, because the CPs had less experience in multicultural environments, and specifically, little experience with ESL students (p. 3). They recommend focusing on tasks and the volunteer skills contributed by ESL students to community needs: "The stereotypes and fear of the Other are soon diminished as people work side-by-side towards a common goal, learning a little more about each other in the process" (p. 3). Use these strategies to maintain positive relationships with your CPs. Be clear about who your group is and what your objectives are. Do your research and ask the volunteer coordinator questions; clear communication shows you are interested in enhancing a healthy partnership (Engaging by Communicating, n.d.).

Keep Commitments

Many CPs are understaffed and their staff members are overworked. Those employed at CPs may be volunteers themselves. If they are paid staff, their pay is oftentimes not substantial. As a teacher, you may have your own time constraints and your students may also be busy. Needless to say, when you commit to an activity, be sure to keep that commitment. When you commit to a certain time, be sure to arrive on time (or a little early), while remembering to account for potential delays. Try to make the most of your time on location so that you maximize the helping hands for the organization. When your volunteer shift is over, move your group out of the way of other volunteer groups or employees trying to complete tasks. Doing these things shows respect for the hard work that people are doing.

Show Gratitude

As an educator, a portion of our work is being the supporter-in-chief. This role does not stop with the CP. Remember to be polite and say *Please* and

Thank you. Express gratitude for the CP for allowing your group the opportunity to help their organization. See Perren (2013) for helpful information about how this can be accomplished. Completing this gratitude step will lead the CP to form a positive opinion of your group as the relationship is refined. Show gratitude to your students for their hard work, too! Doing this will lead them to forming positive opinions of their experiences and a favorable disposition of SL pedagogy and lifelong civic engagement.

Matching Curricular Goals with Community Partnerships

There are at least two types of community partners: (1) large organizations (often non-profit organizations) that you can find in almost every city across the United States (and, in some cases, the world), and (2) smaller, local community organizations. If you have chosen a class theme or two to focus on for the semester, find an organization that has a mission that aligns with your chosen theme. Filter through organizations by looking at the *About Us* section on the organization's website to see if your course themes align with the organization's mission. Then contact the organization's volunteer coordinator and, if possible, visit the location before making a final decision about whether the organization is right for your purpose.

Community Partner Type: Large Organizations

VolunteerMatch (https://www.volunteermatch.org/) and United Way (https://www.unitedway.org/) are great starting points for searching for both large and local organizations. Both websites allow you to search by type of activity. VolunteerMatch also allows you to search for group volunteer activities and has recently started providing increased volunteer matching with online service options as a result of the Covid pandemic and the fact that some SL courses (perhaps most) have moved online.

Habitat for Humanity (https://www.habitat.org/) is an excellent organization to work with if you are just getting started with the idea of TSL. The organization has established experience with volunteer groups, making it simple for SL beginners. With Habitat for Humanity, you can link service to a course theme of homelessness or lack of affordable housing.

American Rivers, The National Rivers Cleanup (https://www.americanrivers.org/) has volunteer opportunities all over the United States. Their website has extensive information about the environment and the importance of conserving clean water, which helps students understand the organization's mission.

Feeding America (https://www.feedingamerica.org/) helps feed those in the United States who are struggling with hunger and caters to large-group activities. Potential course themes that can be linked to Feeding America include food insecurity, food deserts, or nutrition.

Community Partner Type: Smaller Local Community Organizations

Depending on where you are from, the local organizations available for volunteering will vary. Nearly every major city in the United States will have some type of food pantry, which is a good place to start. As mentioned previously with Feeding America, you can tie in popular course themes related to food. Organizing a *drive* event with a local organization is another way to be involved with a local CP. Depending on the organization, you may organize a drive for food, clothing, spices, or childcare supplies. In some areas, there are refugee resettlement programs that need everything from housing staples such as towels and cleaning supplies to furniture. While large organizations have clear plans in place for volunteers (typically sorting produce or moving goods), local food pantries may ask your group to do a wider variety of activities that are unrelated to food. For this reason, you may want to directly ask the volunteer coordinator what types of activities you will do. These types of events can also be easily coordinated with holidays and other civic engagement groups on a college campus or in the community.

Animal shelters are also prominent in many communities. Typically, demand for volunteers at animal shelters is low as it is a popular volunteer location. For this reason, it may be a challenge to find an activity for whole-group service, but if there is someone particularly interested in working with animals, this may be an option. Keep in mind that shelters often have stringent training for volunteers, which may require additional time and training.

Communicate with Volunteer Coordinators

It is very important to maintain clear and regular communication with your community partners. After the research phase and selection of CPs, send an email to the volunteer coordinator at each target CP to help you clarify the parameters of your experience. In this initial email message, provide the number of people in your group and the school you are coming from. Communicating in writing via email will ensure that the organization knows whom to expect along with the dates and times to expect your students. Any misunderstandings can be clarified in writing; the written documentation will also serve as additional administrative purposes. You can also confirm that your class goals and the goals of the CP align, making the experience mutually beneficial. After the initial email communication, consider visiting the CP to meet the volunteer coordinator and see the location. If you are new to TSL, going to the location will be helpful in calming your nerves. During this initial CP visit, you can address any questions or concerns you might have before the service activity takes place.

In addition, consider adding the language proficiency levels of your group in your email communication with the CP representative. Some CPs may even request the language proficiency information in advance. Providing some background information about your group will help the volunteer coordinator be prepared for communicating with them. If listening comprehension levels are low, the people who interact with your group may need to adjust their speaking speed (cf. Perren, 2008). This is a fantastic teaching moment for community members who perhaps have limited experience with ESL students. Different experiences that CPs have with ESL students and their associated English language proficiency is well documented in the literature (Wurr & Perren, 2015). Along with the SL experience for students, we like to think of these interactions as bridging the gap between ESL students and the community. Those individuals that guide you at the CP site gain a better understanding of the ESL community (Askildson et al., 2013; Meier, 2015; Miller & Kostka, 2015), and ESL students gain confidence when speaking to new people (Hummel, 2013; Minor, 2002; Perren, 2013).

Student Behavior and Classroom Management Considerations

A couple of key items to consider are absenteeism, incompatible CP student placements, and excessively involved ESL students at a CP placement or service activity. We suggest you treat absentees in your service-learning courses in the same manner as in traditional courses. If a student is absent and has absences allowed as part of the institution, program, and course, then the student has an occasional pass on attendance. An example policy could be that

ESL students are allowed to be absent from class four absences during the semester with no penalty. Additionally, their final grade will be lowered one notch for each additional class that they miss.

However, you might consider that if a student misses an off-campus SL class session, then that student would be obligated to write a paragraph about the writing or reading assignment that was assigned for that particular day. Ask the student for a well-written explanation about the reading assignment, reason for missing the class, and what they could have learned from that particular on-campus session or volunteer session.

What happens if an ESL student CP placement goes sideways? Well, first of all, that's not good in some respects, but it can also be considered a mechanism for program growth. In that case, you should renegotiate any placement issues by taking into consideration what happened in the particular circumstance and re-adjust as soon as possible. It's a good idea to gather data from all stakeholders in this event and determine the next course of action as has been characterized in other ESL projects (Askildson et al., 2013). This is bound to happen in some TSL courses for a variety of reasons including whether or not the community partner is actually true to its advertisement that it accepts all volunteers, or not (which includes ESL learners of all proficiency levels and ethnic/linguistic backgrounds). One proactive and strategic program-planning initiative is to do one's best to eliminate, reduce, or avoid these types of unfavorable CP placement mismatches. Plan ahead and systematically inquire with students and CP personnel ahead of time regarding what types of social issues or causes they are interested in. We advise this step for better matches for ESL students with their CP placements.

We generally have not experienced many instances of ESL students getting overly involved with questionable behavior at their CP placements. You might have to encourage the student to taper their involvement if burdensome to you, classmates, your institution, or the CP. In that case, it's advisable to simply ask stakeholders (the CP volunteer manager and the student) to give some friendly advice; it might even be your responsibility as part of your job description as the instructor of record. When interacting with a student you can also cite the Student Code of Conduct if need be. We sincerely hope this isn't the case; more information about ESL student behavior and general classroom management techniques is always available (Hafernik et al., 2002; Messerschmitt & Hafernik, 2009). In one specific contrasting example, contrary to what one might expect, it turned out that one of our former ESL students had taken her own initiative to continue visiting the CP placement on her own time to continue participating in volunteer work, to the absolute delight of the CP volunteer manager.

Implementing TESOL Service-Learning with Less Proficient Students

Service-learning can be used to give ESL students opportunities for improving their proficiency. Although English language proficiency issues can be a limiting factor (Ene & Orlando, 2015), there are solutions (Perren & Wurr, 2015; Wendler Shah, 2015). For example, Wendler Shah (2015) describes grouping "international students who had low English proficiency with a student of the same native language who spoke English more confidently, and paired more outgoing students with students who were less vocal in class" (p. 184). At the same time, instructional practices used regularly by ESL teachers in the classroom to address the needs of ESL students with different proficiency levels, not surprisingly, overlap when working out of the classroom. Instructors can group students by proficiency level and then assign them to specific tasks with the CP. Community partnerships are an integral part of improving a SL experience for your students. These partnerships will not only contribute to a thriving community for all, but will also lead your ESL students to feel more connected to the community in which they live. These relationships benefit everyone and may ultimately result in more civic engagement.

Exploration: Unstructured Community Service Activities

Use the steps listed for unstructured activities that students organize themselves.

1. Research CPs that will accept ESL students as individuals, pairs, or groups.
2. Create a list of CPs.
3. Inform students of potential experiences by having them review the *About Us* section of the CPs' websites and other media about the partners (e.g., articles, video clips).
4. Allow students to choose a CP with which they would like to work.
5. Guide students in making a game plan including:
   a. contacting the organization to schedule service activities
   b. planning how they will commute to the location
   c. determining if there is a volunteer manager they can report to and with whom they can officially document the contributed volunteer service/work hours
   d. communicating with each other and the volunteer coordinator.

Exploration: Group Service Activity with a Specific Community Partner

Assisted living communities are great places for a group service activity. This experience tends to be highly interactive and students often express feelings of deep connections from their time there. Use these steps for a group service activity with an assisted living community.

1. *Contact the volunteer coordinator.* Ask about the types of opportunities that exist for ESL students. Depending on the needs of the CP, some experiences with assisted living communities may require little preparation as they are looking for students simply to sit and chat with residents. Other times, they would like students to create presentations to give to small groups of residents who are interested in listening.

2. *Ask about special information.* You might need to know about the residents to prepare students and avoid potentially uncomfortable or challenging circumstances. For example, you might ask if the residents are in a memory-loss center. This information shapes how you should prepare your students.

3. *Prepare your students for working with this population.* Provide background information about assisted living facilities (as these living situations are less common in some cultures), as well as information about whom they will be interacting with, what they will be expected to do, and why they are completing this activity. Encourage students to ask questions. This item and the next three all relate to adequate pre-departure preparation.

4. *Teach strategies for interacting and communicating while on site.* Look for online articles that provide useful tips for interacting with this population. Often these articles are for communicating with elderly family members, so you will probably need to adapt the readings to be more suitable for your class depending on your ESL students' proficiency levels. A good launching point is the article "How to communicate effectively with older adults" (Ni, 2014).

5. *Talk about boundaries.* This includes avoiding physical contact, not taking photos or videos, and maintaining confidentiality. Again, consider cultural differences to make this service experience most comfortable for all involved. There might also be a requirement that no photos or video be taken at your community partner site (with a signed waiver!).

6. *Prepare for the service.* If creating cultural presentations, you may want to practice sharing them in class so that students are more comfortable when the time comes to give the presentation.

7. *Complete the SL activity.* On the day of the activity, remind the students of the communication strategies and boundaries discussed. After the service activity has ended (while still on the CP site), take a few minutes as a group to verbally reflect on the experience (see Chapter 4, "Assessment in TESOL Service-Learning," for further discussion of this type of unstructured reflection activity). It is always nice to hear immediate feedback from students when adrenaline is still high.

Exploration: Group Gratitude Activity—The Thank-You Card Process

Writing thank-you cards may seem like a dying practice, but they teach students about U.S. culture and also helps them prepare for other situations in which writing a thank-you note may be helpful. Follow these steps to teach some of this etiquette to your students.

1. Explain the cultural importance of a thank-you note, along with the typical structure used. Here is a list of the items to include: greeting, expression of thanks, specific details, look ahead, restatement of thanks, ending with your regards (Field, 2016).
   a. Greeting (*Dear _____*)
   b. Expression of Gratitude (*Thank you so much for....*)
   c. Details (*Here is a picture of our class volunteering at your organization.*)
   d. Looking Forward (*We look forward to volunteering with you again.*)
   e. Restatement of Gratitude (*Thank you again for providing us with this experience.*)
   f. Regards (*Many thanks,*)
2. Provide a few sample phrases to get the class started with a greeting. Remind students to double-check that they use the correct form and spelling of the person's name as well as anyone else's name mentioned in the note.
3. Ask students to begin with the two most important words: *Thank you.* They can show their gratitude by explicitly thanking the recipient for the experience.

4. Encourage students to provide details by telling the recipients how they plan to use their collaboration as a learning experience. It shows them that they really appreciate the thought that went into it.
5. Even if students integrate minor learning points, encourage them to describe how they will present the valuable learning points to others in the community. For example, it might include statements like: *Here's a picture of us at your site. We look so professional! We can't wait to use the important learning points you provided to...* or *This experience meant so much to us. Having all of our class working together with your staff in one place was something we'll never forget.*
   Tell students to mention the next time they might see them or just let them know that they are thinking of them. For example, *We look forward to seeing you next month at your next planned event.*
6. Encourage students to restate their appreciation and to add details to thank their CP in a different way. For example, *Again, thank you for your generosity. We're so excited about visiting your site again. We'll let you know all about it when we get our schedule organized.*
7. Show students how to end the card with their regards. *Sincerely* is a safe standby, but for closer relationships, they might choose a warmer option. Talk about the different ways to finish a letter and how different levels of intimacy are expressed in these closing phrases.
8. Ask students to write the cards to the CPs visited during the duration of the course. This includes having all students sign each card, putting the address of the CP in the correct location on the envelope, and placing the postage stamp (purchased ahead of time by either you or students). This is a great opportunity to teach formatting of envelopes, as some students may not have filled out their own envelopes before.
9. Mail the thank-you cards to the CP.

3. I'm Ready...Now What Do I Teach?

You have thought about ways to connect your curricular goals and themes to service-learning (SL) activities and have found and communicated with community partners (CPs) who will help you achieve these goals. Now what should you do from an instructional standpoint with SL? Fortunately, SL is very adaptable; you can truly teach whatever you'd like. You will need a syllabus, lesson planning, and assignments and activities. Furthermore, the foundational parts of language teaching—reading, writing, speaking, and listening—are always good teaching options. There are also many ESL content possibilities beyond these which are indicated in this section. The activities described are just a few examples of the type of instruction that you can do through SL. Many of these topics overlap and are difficult to place into just one category. Hence, you need to be flexible in how these topics can be applied to the traditional four language learning skills as well as how they can be applied to teaching grammar and vocabulary, etc. Moreover, given the scope and content limitations of this publication, we are not attempting an overly ambitious treatment of every possible pedagogical opportunity with service-learning.

Please be aware that current and expanding information for running a TESOL service-learning course remotely is important, since virtual instruction has become commonplace. ESL teachers will likely need to re-adjust their activities and assessment tools according to the particular configuration that they will use for instructional delivery, whether virtual or otherwise. Operating TSL courses remotely (and many courses in general) has been happening at institutions around the world. Some of the constraints for remote TSL delivery with ESL students relate to the fact that many programs and educators are simply not pursuing these options, or are unable to because of (1) a dramatic reduction of international student enrollment in the United States, (2) more stringent visa restrictions imposed by government policy, and (3) fewer service opportunities available that correspond with ESL course and curricular requirements.

However, there are more available resources for remote delivery of TSL service-learning courses as shared throughout this ebook. After you create a syllabus and decide on learning objectives, learning tasks and activities, and assessment practices (which are presented next in this chapter), you can review and select interesting and promising technology-related apps and websites for second language learning (Guillén et al., 2020). This is because technology is currently being used creatively to teach language during the COVID-19 crisis with increased intentional connections between language users that is based on "empathetic human contact with others in this crisis" (Guillén et al., 2020, p. 2). This is also good news because these educational practices of using technology for remote delivery coincide with the TESOL Technology Standards framework for virtual learning (Healey et al., 2011). One reassuring element of that connection is the importance of using specific technology types to accomplish learning objectives of any course rather than for the sake of using technology because it is technology.

Specific Methods of Including Service-Learning in ESL Courses

Combine ESL and Service-Learning for Your Community Engagement Syllabus

Let's now turn to specifically describing a TSL course that starts from an ESL content course. ESL reading content courses, ESL listening and speaking content courses, etc., are examples of ESL content courses taught in Intensive English Programs, Academic English Programs, and community colleges. Our suggestions are to start from those ESL content courses and add several service-learning educational objectives to coincide with the ESL content learning objectives depending on whether you are teaching writing, listening and speaking, reading, etc. Therefore, your syllabus is an essential component of a TSL course for teaching ESL content. There are four elements that are required for creating any course syllabus for ESL instruction, including when you use SL as the pedagogy: goals, learning objectives, topics, assessment (Graves, 2014; Echevarria et al., 2017). Table 3.1 shows examples of these separate elements. The manner in which you modify your own particular TSL syllabus based on ESL content has many possibilities. One way to get started with this is to explore and experiment, take a step back and evaluate, and then re-structure and try again.

Please include a timeline and schedule for activities and events, as this element is especially important when planning events that occur off-campus as fieldwork or as virtual volunteering options. The number of events you

Table 3.1 Four Elements in a TSL Syllabus

Goals	Learning Objectives	Topics	Assessment
• Enhance critical-thinking and interpersonal skills • Develop a better understanding of course content • Advance academic performance and retention • Promote learning through active participation	• Participate in hands-on experiential active learning in listening/speaking situations outside the classroom • Engage in responsible and challenging actions for the common good • Reflect critically on the service experience	• Homelessness in America • Food Scarcity • Senior Citizens • Environment • Incarceration • Race Relations	• Attendance and Participation 15% • Reflection Writings 20% • Formal Assessments 30% • Oral Presentation 15% • ESL Day of Service Project 10% • Homework 10%

decide to hold depends on a multitude of factors that will have a lot to do with how organized you are and the needs of the community partner. Despite that, extensive description in this ebook of the number of virtual events an ESL teacher can schedule is beyond the scope of this limited publication space. The syllabus ideas mentioned primarily target higher education settings. However, K–12 syllabus design options structured around English language are available and can be readily adapted for SL (Echevarria et al., 2017). A sample syllabus is located in Appendix A.

Lesson Planning

Once a TSL syllabus has been created, it's time to integrate TSL lesson planning. Construct your written lesson plan carefully since experienced teachers attest to using written lesson plans. There are options available though, since "a written lesson plan can be as simple as a few notes or quite formal, with each step written out in detail" (Weigle, 2014, p. 230). Be sure to construct a suitable TSL lesson plan that includes relevant community engagement concepts discussed so far. We suggest that you include these essential elements in your TSL lesson plan tied to an ESL course: background, procedures, follow-up, and notes (Purgason, 2014). Several sample assignments and activities for TSL lesson plans for an ESL course can be found in Appendix B.

Decide on Various Types of Class and Group Configurations for Service Activities

Whole-Class Activities

Organizing a service activity that the entire class attends is perhaps the simplest activity type to arrange. Once you have established community partnerships (see Chapter 2, "Strategies for Successful Community Partnerships"), the legwork is minimal. First, decide what type of experience and how much interaction you would like for your students. For example, if you would like a highly interactive experience in which students are verbally communicating most of the time, an assisted living center might be better than participating during a shift at a Habitat for Humanity construction project site, or a resale store—not all service experiences are created equal. Familiarize yourself with direct and indirect service types (Community Engagement, 2020) to help make that decision, and be sure to consider your student learning outcomes to ensure a positive and worthwhile experience.

Transportation is one potential challenge to the whole-class SL activity (see Perren, 2013). Consider the travel time to and from the activity; a whole SL class can be completed as just a one-day or one-time event as a capstone activity related to the class theme, several times at different community partner locations, or with one community partner several times (Bippus & Eslami, 2013). Again, whichever class and group configuration for service activities you decide on should be coordinated closely with your course learning objectives, available transportation, and time schedule. Use these basic steps to set up and complete a SL activity with any CP.

1. Decide what you would like students to learn from the experience as you are researching CPs that accept groups of your size.
2. Contact potential CPs via email or phone, and, if possible, visit the CP site location before you bring your class.
3. Prepare students for the experience by having them review the *About Us* section of the CP's website and other media about the partner (e.g., articles, video clips).
4. Discuss expectations for the service to be completed with the CP coordinator and with the class, the expectations not related to L2 learning and give examples of proper clothing, student conduct, etc., before visiting and while at the partner site.
5. Complete the SL experience and finish with a structured or unstructured (and required) reflective activity or assignment.

Structured Group Activities (Several Groups Who Commit to One Community Partner)

Ask several groups within your class to commit to one CP for the duration of the class. This option creates more connections in the community; allows for student autonomy; and, by sharing information and their experiences in the classroom, makes the students the experts in certain areas. Structured group activities may create a bit more work for instructors, as it necessitates increased monitoring of students to ensure that learning outcomes are being met and also opens the door for potential miscommunication and transportation issues. To avoid these issues, establish easy ways to get in touch quickly. If you are not comfortable creating a group text with your personal phone number, consider using popular mobile messaging applications such as WhatsApp, Kakaotalk, WeChat, and Line that international and ESL students are likely already using.

Structured Group Activities in Which Students Self-Select Community Partners

Asking students to self-select the CP they would like to work with makes the service they complete more personal and meaningful. Use the steps listed to create activities in which students self-select CPs.

1. Contact potential partners via email or phone and visit site locations prior to attendance.
2. Create a list of CPs, times that assistance is needed, and what type of work the students are likely to do.
3. Inform students of potential experiences by asking them to review the *About Us* section of the CPs' websites and other media about the partners (e.g., articles, video clips).
4. Allow students to choose the CP with which they would like to work.
5. Guide students in making a game plan that organizes how the group will commute to the location, as well as communicate with each other and the volunteer coordinator.

Unstructured Service (Students Must Complete a Specified Number of Hours per Semester)

Depending on both the language and the comfort level of students, promoting unstructured service activities may be appropriate in your teaching situation. Unstructured activities require that the instructor give up some control and spend more time monitoring from a distance. Students complete this volunteer service independently; in this situation, a certain number of service hours is required per semester depending on the course. This model more closely follows general SL courses connected to academic departments that have been utilizing this practice for several decades. Many colleges and universities list the number of required volunteer service hours on their websites:

- California State University/Long Beach: 20 hours during the semester (1–2 hours per week): http://www.csulb.edu/center-for-community-engagement
- Red Rocks Community College: 15 hours per term: https://www.rrcc.edu/sites/default/files/u2757/Service%20Learning%20Handbook_final.doc
- San Jose State University: 10 hours per semester: http://www.sjsu.edu/gup/ugs/faculty/curriculum/servicelearning/index.html

The number of hours of service per semester varies depending on the number of academic credits for your specific course; making the total number of hours clear from the beginning of the course and instigating a mechanism for tracking these ESL student service hours will help you avoid potential misunderstandings.

Teaching Various Types of ESL Content in TSL Courses

Now that the information is available for creating a syllabus, lesson planning, and making activities, the discussion now moves to teaching various types of relevant content for ESL-related courses. Here, suggestions are offered for using TSL methodology to introduce culture, vocabulary, aspects of spoken language, and technology.

Culture

Culture can be taught during pre-service activities and can be utilized for the purpose of achieving course learning objectives related to culture, literacy, and vocabulary. Before working with any CPs, ensure that students are well-informed and prepared for what to expect in a specific CP location by reading about the type of work the organization does. Through these readings, students learn about U.S. culture—and that of the CP as well. The focus of culture can also correspond to your utilization of teaching materials based on the cultures of your students. As a teacher, you can have your students create cultural presentations related to their particular ethnic and linguistic backgrounds to share with community partners in different capacities. This would provide opportunities for exchange of culture and ideas. Clearly, it is important to teach culture in ESL service-learning courses given that "L2 students in colleges and universities in the United States, Canada, and other English-speaking countries do not always follow the norms of politeness and appropriate-ness commonly accepted in their L2 communities" (Hinkel, 2014, p. 397). You can try out tasks in your ESL service-learning course that focus on culture by training students to carefully observe people and their interactions at CP sites during service. You can also create basic checklists of culturally appropriate and common interaction routines.

You might also instruct your ESL students in how to pay attention to linguistic expressions and vocabulary items used between people of different genders, ages, linguistic backgrounds, and occupational roles at CP sites. You can have students compare the information they collect in these service assignments to English language teaching materials found in video interviews on YouTube, textbooks, and standardized testing materials, etc. Your teaching repertoire for including cultural content for ESL service-learning could also include having students involved in role-play activities or brief acting activities, with spoken audio or video recordings (with written scripts) that focus on communicative interactions that took place at CP sites. Many of these activities can be adjusted for learner proficiency level. Currently, available resources offer a repository of additional information for teaching culture in ESL service-learning courses (Perren & Wurr, 2015).

Vocabulary

For an ESL educator, there is great potential for teaching vocabulary when using service-learning. We definitely see that vocabulary is critical in teaching and learning a language, because vocabulary knowledge is a central foundation for all learners and communication. This is especially true for ESL service-learning, because of the nature of the high stakes and authentic communication involved when students participate in volunteer service activities. Besides curated readings related to culture or a CP organization, students may also skim and scan the CP's website to locate and define unknown vocabulary, which provides students with online search experiences while you assist them in finding answers to questions that they have about the CP. It is important to make sure that students know not only the vocabulary related to the CP, but also commonly used phrases they may need to do CP work. Ask the CP volunteer coordinator/manager to provide a list of frequently asked questions that you can share with students from a vocabulary standpoint. These lists of questions and words can then be adapted using a variety of established vocabulary learning resources (Coxhead, 2014; Nation, 2001). Options for teaching vocabulary with service-learning are readily available *and* advised since "it is unlikely that any language learner ever wished he or she had a smaller vocabulary" (Coxhead, 2014, p. x).

Spoken Language

In TESOL and applied linguistics, "speaking is considered by many to be the fundamental skill in second language (L2) learning" (Lazaraton, 2014, p. 106). Furthermore, many of our service-learning ESL activities align with the notion that "second language skills are best learned if speaking is a major component of the learning process" (Khan, 2017). Hence, since speaking is a specific skill, we also know that speaking can be combined productively with any of the other traditional three skills. TSL research has also reported on benefits of developing speaking skills through community SL (Hummel, 2013; Perren, 2013; Steinke, 2009). For example, Hummel (2013) discusses the use of SL to enhance language acquisition through authentic and non-threatening social interactions.

Nonetheless, in academic English programs, educators do not always have time to focus on informal speaking. If you choose an SL activity that requires a lot of verbal communication, consider pre-teaching some interactional skills such as turn-taking, eliciting information, asking for clarification, and making small talk. These speaking functions correspond with learning how to interact with others in two-way (participatory) listening (Goh, 2014). You can teach these combined skills as part of service tasks in the classroom or in coordination with on-site CP experiences (pre-, during, and after service). Examples of learning activities for spoken participation are tasks in which students discuss a particular type of problem. You can also direct your ESL students to practice listening skills in discussions by focusing on differentiating between main ideas and details. The information ESL students gather from this type of task could also be transferred to speaking activities and skill reinforcement in spoken language by sharing their opinions and making recommendations (Goh, 2014). These learning opportunities enable ESL students to offer solutions.

In communicative situations such as at a CP site or in a SL classroom, teach your ESL students *clarification questions* such as "Could you say that again, please?" This is so ESL students in SL courses can "learn to use cooperation strategies to help improve their comprehension" by pre-teaching relevant clarification questions and phrases learners can utilize for seeking assistance (Goh, 2014, p. 81). Teaching clarification questions is a must, because SL activities are often new experiences for students while they are out of their comfort zone. Students need to feel comfortable asking questions if they do not understand the instructions from the CP.

The skills you can teach with the information above are also practical life-skills for ESL students, who may lack confidence in communicating with new people. Examples for teaching how to ask clarification questions can be found in existing ESL resource materials (Oxford, 1990; Perren 2012). For example, one way to prepare is with the use of *table tents* (popular in restaurant dining rooms) as classroom learning materials (Perren, 2012). Simple pieces of paper serve as reminders for students to use specific language. They can include template sentences and questions for ESL students to discuss reading materials and ask questions for clarification. You can promote deeper understanding during real-time communication by teaching ESL students in service-learning contexts to ask questions for clarification.

Teaching these interactional skills is a great way to practice strategies that build community connections and students' networking capabilities, especially when using the target language—English. Using English in mixed L1 groups as classroom management and community-service tasks is something each of us has experienced and a topic that has received attention in TSL (Askildson et al., 2013; Verner, n.d.). Although we support the use of the L1 when students interact in groups and in class, in SL situations we perceive the use of English as particularly important. Of course, the SL context is well-suited to giving international students an opportunity to use English in a non-academic setting, but using English is even more critical when there are others in the CP setting who might not understand a conversation in a language other than English. Unfortunately, in some cases, the CP and clients they serve might find world languages off-putting due to limited exposure and the feeling of being left out. For these reasons, we suggest that ESL teachers structure classroom and field activities using English as much as possible.

Small Talk for Informal Speaking and Listening

Small-talk topics or even the concept of small talk may feel awkward or unfamiliar for ESL students in community-based SL activities. Initiating and maintaining small talk is important for ESL learners to create connections with others (Holmes, 2000). Consider including some lighter, socially oriented, speaking activities before, during, and after the planned volunteer community service tasks. These activities can be as structured as needed. Perren (2013) has suggested a format that employs lists of pre-printed conversation points that align with spoken language learning objectives consistent with "conversation strategies found in listening- and speaking-oriented English language education materials" (p. 499). The SL course setting provides excellent situations for practicing small talk, which, along with work-related communication, is perceived by L2 users of English as beneficial and necessary (Perren, 2007). How to initiate a conversation, what topics are appropriate for small talk, and how to exit a conversation, are practical skills for international and ESL students.

Pragmatics

Pragmatics, which often takes a back seat in ESL programs and courses (Louw et al., 2010; Zeldenrust, 2017) is "the social language skills we use in our communicative interactions with others" (Zeldenrust, 2017, p. 2). TESOL service-learning scholars have been interested in pragmatics for practical reasons, including intercultural development (Avineri, 2015), civic engagement program development training (Askildson et al., 2013), and ESL literacy (Crossman & Kite, 2007). You can emphasize pragmatic learning in your ESL teaching by directing learner attention toward traditional speech acts, such as greetings, compliments, and complaints; this can be accomplished through pair and group activities and assessments (Leung & Lewkowicz, 2006). Using a pragmatics focus provides ESL students in SL experiences with essential language and intercultural knowledge, such as how to interpret when someone is making a request versus giving you a choice (*Do you wanna help move this furniture?*). Not only do students learn these pragmatic communicative skills, but they also begin or augment their ability to recognize issues of inequity. Then, you can help your ESL students build on their developing knowledge, skills, and attitudes toward social justice in problem solving with socioculturally appropriate language use.

You are encouraged to use pragmatic activities in your TSL courses and show YouTube video/movie excerpts from news media and TV programs (Hinkel, 2014). Sometimes useful videos can be located on CP websites. The internet provides an ever-growing wealth of video resources that permit you to teach your ESL students about how culture can influence language use with examples of formulaic language, requests, and routine interactions (such as service encounters, body language, turn-taking, and more). Ask your students to gather information about acceptable language used in their community that meets sociocultural and politeness expectations. As a teacher you can then plan SL lessons with learning activities such as role plays, presentations, and writing assignments. In these assignments, you can include information about English speech acts and politeness routines that use certain words or expressions discovered in video clips (Hinkel, 2014). Students can then make comparisons between what they find on the internet and the language taking place at CP organization sites. To sum up, although beyond the scope of this current publication, additional research is available regarding the intersection of second language learning and use, pragmatics, directives, and requests (Cardellio, 2016; Fioramonte, 2014; Perren, 2008).

Technology

We thought it prudent to acknowledge that technology is not considered an "ESL content area" as other content areas we have mentioned (i.e., reading, grammar, etc.). We do advise ESL teachers to think about how important technology is to ESL education, and these days with the push to virtual instruction due to the Covid-19 pandemic. That is the reason for us to include information about how you can coordinate your ESL teaching with technology.

For the past 25 years, TESOL scholars have discussed technology in SL with articles about writing development and the internet (Warschauer, 1996; Warschauer & Cook, 1999), influences on motivation, teaching of internet skills to children, and production of web pages for community organizations. As it was previously mentioned, the importance of using technology also aligns with the TESOL Technology Standards framework for using technology to accomplish specific ESL learning objectives. Related research discusses implementation of technology as part of using SL for L2 learning (Bickel et al., 2013; Maloy et al., 2015; Meier, 2015; Purmensky, 2009). These reports describe SL projects and the English language learning needs of a variety of students in conjunction with technology. There are specific opportunities for the use of technology with CPs in which the CP needs technology assistance. And there are equally available opportunities for ESL students to learn ESL content knowledge. In these cases, learning the ESL content through SL with technology is useful to accomplish those aims. For example, Maloy and colleagues (2015) report on a college ESL digital storytelling project about human rights issues and its long-term effects on student development; they highlight an increased sense of belonging and self-worth among the ESL students, because they contributed valuable information to the university community. Also of relevance in TSL research is the high-impact practices in ESL literacy courses as part of a balanced curriculum that promote both civic engagement and provide writing exam preparation (Maloy et al., 2015).

When integrating remote learning, relying only on Zoom might not help ESL students accomplish their learning goals in a SL course. ESL teachers are advised to utilize a combination of software apps with cell phones that might offer more productive and dynamic options for students. There are ways to run a virtual service-learning course using technology that allow ESL students to engage in civic action in their communities. Here are a couple of illustrations for how technology is also being used during the Covid pandemic. One teacher's ESL students were recently involved in communicating with technology "through petitions and social media engagement" (Guillén et al., 2020, p. 7), by focusing them on issues of immigrants' rights in detention facilities during Covid. Other remote TSL possibilities have structured ESL activities based on older and traditional teaching ideas matching students with student teachers. For instance, a teacher can run a virtual course by pairing ESL students through Zoom with conversation partners in graduate teaching programs (K. Purmensky, personal communication, October 21, 2020). Another way to integrate online volunteering with a specific software application is to ask students to sign up with the organization Be My Eyes at its website (Bemyeyes.com). Student volunteers can then find out how to download a software application (app) on their cell phones so they can participate as a volunteer. The organization's goal is that "sighted volunteers lend their eyes to solve tasks big and small to help blind and low-vision people lead more independent lives" (Be My Eyes, 2020).

Publishing on the internet, or *web publishing* (Christensson, 2011), is an excellent activity for TSL (Warschauer & Cook, 1999). Web publishing can be taught through personal or class websites, blogs, tweets, comments, or a more formal newsletter. These structured learning activities foster cooperative student work, adding to both authorial voice and audience awareness. By assigning ESL students to explore and write about SL-sensitive topics, rather than simply another required writing prompt, ESL educators can create an empowering writing experience. In addition, micropublishing enables English language learners to learn how to use their writing skills to express themselves with SL reflections. You can also teach students to expand academic writing skills by using the internet to share information about CPs. Furthermore, this type of writing assignment can be closely connected to the TESOL Technology Standards for learners (Healey et al, 2011). An ESL teacher can find ways to get the ESL students involved in writing publication copy for CP organizations (such as CP promotional materials) as part of indirect service activities.

Exploration: Community Engagement and the Environment

Ask learners to engage in a collaborative in-class reading experience followed by an out-of-class visit to a neighborhood park, beach, etc., for an environment clean-up project (e.g., Make a Difference Day project). Use both pre-reading and during-reading strategies (Nation, 2009) to practice reading and writing about (1) content related to community engagement with a specific type of environmental issue, and (2) information about spoken communication strategies. In other words, focus on teaching active reading strategies while also recognizing appropriate ways of communicating with CP volunteer managers as well as other volunteers and employees that may be involved in the tasks. Researchers have found that communication about both work-related and social topics while completing volunteer work is beneficial for international speakers of English (Perren, 2007). Use the steps listed below as an in-class activity prior to service for supporting students' community engagement with the environment.

1. Require students to read and respond to reading material about the environment, using pre-reading and during-reading skills as part of their preparation for community engagement field experiences.
2. Ask students to listen carefully to instructions for the proposed activity and to ask questions to clarify potential misunderstandings about the reading and the CP service.
3. To make the activity more interactive, invite students to set their own conversational goals for the duration of the activity (e.g., speak to a new person, make small talk with a classmate) based on common academic communication strategies (Oxford, 1990).
4. Assign students to groups.
5. Pass out a reading article about environment clean-up projects.
6. Ask students to collaborate on interaction and prediction strategies.
   a. Ask students to skim through the article for about five minutes.
   b. Write on the board possible questions asking about key facts:
      i. What is the main purpose of environmental protection for the public?

      ii. What are some main types of environment clean-up projects?
      iii.Who are the main participants of environment clean-up projects
         in your area?

7. Ask students to find out key facts about protecting the environment
   in the United States or in a close geographical area. Pair up the
   students and ask each pair to find the answer to the three questions
   from Step 6 together.
   a. Call on pairs to list their answers on the board.
   b. Encourage students to share their answers with the class and add
      more details about an idea for an environment clean-up project.
   c. Explain vocabulary whenever it is necessary.
8. Tell students that they are going to go to a city or county park or beach
   in their local community.
9. Assign students to complete the remainder of the reading
   as homework.

This activity also teaches learners to recognize specific vocabulary and topics related to the environment when communicating with various people at
a CP site.

Exploration: Spoken Language Activity with Instructions

Share with students the nature of the CP function and the volunteer tasks
to be completed. Pre-teach integral vocabulary and phrases that students are
likely to hear. Explain that instructions will be given to the main group by a
volunteer manager or a CP representative. Inform students that they will be
expected to break into teams and that one person from each group will repeat
the previous instructions for the team. Use these steps to set up and complete
a spoken language activity with instructions.

1. Communicate with the CP volunteer manager ahead of time to ask
   about the type of tasks students will be completing and what type of
   instructions will be given.
2. Ask the CP volunteer manager if there is any written form of the oral
   instructions that you can receive in advance to review with students.
3. Require students to take brief notes; this can be the responsibility of
   one or two group members. This can also be done in groups with one
   notetaker and one instruction repeater.

4. Ask students to listen carefully to the volunteer manager's instructions and follow along with the students. Allow students to ask questions and verify their understanding before you ask questions. (This technique works well in the classroom too!)
5. Put students in groups and separate them into different locations of the work area for private group work. Choose a leader for each group.
6. Instruct the leaders and note-takers to collaborate and verify their understanding of instructions.
7. Check the accuracy of the instructions before beginning the community service tasks.
8. Modify the instructions or this activity as necessary, based on student comprehension and ability to provide accurate repeated oral instructions.

Exploration: Digital Literacy and Internet Publication Activity

Creating class internet publications such as newsletters and brochures for a SL class is a fun and effective way for English language learners to refine their language and digital literacy skills as they learn vocabulary through writing and interacting with others.

Use these steps for teaching a micropublishing activity in a SL class:

1. Provide reading material and newsletter of brochure publication templates.
2. Link the assignment to the TESOL Technology Standards for learners.
3. Ask students to create a list of publication topics (pre-departure, content, volunteer spotlight, community partner focus, etc.).
4. Assign students to groups to co-author an article or page of articles, either individually written, or co-written.
5. Require students to write, read, respond to, and edit their own and others' articles.
6. Prompt students to include age-appropriate graphics to match their article content.
7. Direct students to share their newsletter.

This exploration is a multi-phase capstone activity that allows students from different cultural backgrounds to find common ground and work cooperatively in civic engagement activities. Students can improve their writing through several drafts and revisions. Moreover, when TESOL educators combine SL activities and internet publication, students learn the benefits of teamwork and experience ownership after seeing the result—an actual publication.

The goals of creating a publication for a SL project and course are to (1) enable ESL students to share their reflective experiences with volunteering and civic engagement fieldwork online, and (2) to bring the ESL classroom community together as competent international users of English. Through micropublishing, students express themselves through their writing and internet design abilities. By completing these service-learning activities, ESL students also transfer the experience they gain through teamwork and other skills to help them with future career and job opportunities.

4. Assessment in TESOL Service-Learning

Let's first discuss traditional assessment in service-learning as written reflection (Kolb, 1984; Zlotkowski, 1998) and the need to understand and teach with various forms of assessment for civic engagement. Then, the ways that written reflection for ESL/EFL learners have been integrated into TSL and community engagement contexts will be discussed, followed by ideas on how to integrate the assessment of socially situated language-in-use with service-learning. We also provide an example of how a teacher could apply SL assessment information with ESL students in the classroom.

Pioneers of SL have discussed the challenges of creating concepts for assessing what is learned through off-campus experiential learning (Stanton et al., 1999, pp. 159–163). They struggled with this until about 1977, when David Kolb directed attention to the *necessary skills* concept of observation, reflection, interpretation, and analysis. Kolb specifically emphasized that teaching students to learn from experience was developing the skill of observation so that "students know the difference between observing and *making snap judgments* about what they saw" (Stanton et al., 1999, p. 161, emphasis added). Hence, written reflection directed at accurate observation eventually became the standardized assessment practice in SL (Kolb, 1984; Zlotkowski, 1998). Assessment (and reflection) in SL has been described as a combination of knowledge and expertise needed for developing and understanding the impact of SL (Gelmon et al., 2001). Increased involvement of SL practitioners in assessment results in beneficial collaborations between faculty members from a variety of institutions. A more pronounced professional engagement in SL assessment scholarship and research can lead to beneficial contextualization of assessment practices. A list of service-learning assessment resources is found in Appendix C.

Understanding Service-Learning and Reflection as Assessment

One prominent feature of successful SL programs is the systematic reflection by learners of their experiences. SL engages students in "meaningful community service that is linked to students' academic experience through related course materials and reflective activities" (Zlotkowski, 1998, p. 3). Written reflection improves learning quality by structuring students' continuous examination of their field experiences in critical ways. You are encouraged to try this in your ESL courses by discussing learning outcomes during informal situations and then directing your ESL students to transfer those ideas into formal and organized writing. The results from a SL written reflection promote foundational experiences, which become the basis for learning. This initial basis forms the central and intentional reflection components that promote deep and meaningful learning that is based on service-learning research from theorists such as John Dewey, David Kolb, and others. They believe that people learn deeply through repeated and continuous cycles of action and reflection (Jacoby, 2003).

Written Reflection Assessment in TESOL Contexts

A number of scholars have explored the topic of assessment as a key part of TESOL Service-Learning (TSL) (Askildson et al., 2013; Bickel et al., 2013; Crossman & Kite, 2007; Perren, 2013; Perren et al., 2013; Purmensky, 2009; Wurr, 1999, 2002). The most common standard practice in TSL is the use of written student reflections for assessment of language proficiency (Crossman & Kite, 2007; Purmensky, 2009; Wurr, 1999, 2002). Written reflections in TSL also show evidence of: (1) how students' ideas about social issues evolve, (2) a focus on assessment to further strengthen SL pedagogy, and (3) the prioritization of the SL assessment process through written reflections as indispensable in TSL (Purmensky, 2009; Wurr, 1999, 2002). Related TSL research supports combining written reflection assessment with additional elements such as formative language assessment and computer-based testing (Perren, 2013; Perren et al., 2013), use of online social networking sites such as Facebook and video-conferencing software (Bickel et al., 2013; Purmensky, 2015), and digital mentoring (Purmensky, 2009, 2015). These studies show us that assessment is at the forefront of key foundational elements of TSL. This is particularly important because research reports of this nature explain how to assess ESL students with a variety of valid and reliable assessment measurements agreed-upon by professionals in our field. Please consider reviewing some of these research reports and making connections to the short exploration activities outlined in this section. We are all obligated to provide relevant and legitimate assessment data about the progress of our ESL students as part of the assessment process. Practical assessment of ESL teaching materials and assessment research exemplify how you can collect and monitor ESL student progress and what you need as an ESL teacher to complete the assessment process. We are limited with this ebook on providing more than cursory information about assessment. It is very likely though, that as instructors of record, you are routinely encouraged in your ESL programs and courses to adequately explain student progress with language proficiency and related content.

Structured and Unstructured Reflection: Before, During, and After Service

TSL makes room for both structured and unstructured reflective and assessment activities. Although not a prominent nor well-understood concept in TSL, scholars have examined various circumstances in which either option may be a beneficial addition to a battery of reflection assessments (Billig & Eyler, 2003; Bringle, 2003; Bringle et al., 2011). One interpretation is that structured reflection activities may assist novice SL students, while unstructured reflection activities could be better for experienced SL students (Bringle, 2003). Thus, the impact of the type of reflection on learning to some degree "depends on the background of the learner" (Bringle, 2003, p. 11).

ESL teachers can choose among numerous potential testing and measurement tasks. Widely used approaches to implementing structured written reflection are through the continuous process of reflecting before, during, and after community-based volunteer service activities and tasks. One reflection framework (of many available) is the DEAL Model for critical reflection that asks students to Describe experiences objectively, Examine experiences vis-à-vis personal growth, civic learning, and academic enhancement, and then Articulate Learning (Ash & Clayton, 2009). When reflection is the core of SL in any discipline, it plays a key role in systematically measuring students' deeper understanding of their learning through community engagement. With the instructor's guidance, it can also help learners expand critical-thinking skills.

Additional assessment research discusses the benefit of unstructured and/or spontaneous reflection in ESL settings:

> Oral reflection was embedded into every class to prepare and debrief students on their service, asking questions to test their understanding of an organization's mission, infrastructure, programming, and success in achieving stated goals. Peer facilitators also used travel time to and from the sites for this purpose.
>
> (Askildson et al., 2013, p. 414)

Our own anecdotal experiences have also repeatedly shown benefits of using unstructured reflection for a range of issues concerning ESL and graduate TESOL students' SL experiences. One specific type of unstructured reflection question is provided here. During or immediately after a volunteer field service experience, a teacher can ask this question: *What connections can you make between the community partner mission statement we previously read about and the volunteer service we completed today?* These immediate reflections provide an informal and conversational way to address linguistic misunderstandings and more deeply understand the social issues that the CP is addressing. For example, Perren (2013) describes the use of "a series of conversation strategies found in listening and speaking-oriented English language education materials" (p. 499), that served as pre-departure language warm-ups and debriefings during transportation to and from CP sites. In other words, specific phrases and vocabulary were provided for students to practice language while on their way to and from the non-profit organization where they engaged in community service. These were basically general English expressions and phrases (Kisslinger, 2000). For example, Strategy 1: Asking for Help in a Conversation, introduced ESL students to the idea that "Sometimes in a conversation, you need a word you did not know. Here are some useful ways to ask for help:

- What does _____ mean?
- How do you use _____ in a sentence?
- What's another word for _____?" (Kisslinger, 2000, p. 64)

You can print these template phrases off in copies or upload them to a learning app, such as Nearpod (mentioned in the Exit Ticket Exploration) for discussion during transit to CP locations. These unrehearsed conversations often took the form of spoken reflection indicating that they can also be used by students to begin the drafting process of a more formal written reflection.

Integrating Ideas for Socially Situated Language-In-Use

It's important to discuss theory-grounded assessment issues in the TESOL field (e.g., ideology, power, identity, dominance) and offer practical and hands-on approaches to those issues in classrooms and communities (Avineri & Perren, 2019). Socially situated language is an increasingly important issue in the field of language testing. Avineri and Perren's (2019) interpretation of assessment trends is presented for TSL language testing. It discusses assessment of communicative language, pragmatics, interculturality, authenticity, washback, and social considerations. The socially situated approach (Avineri & Perren, 2019) to language-in-use incorporates seven features:

1. Sensitivity to context (assessment is relational, not individual)
2. Recognition of ideologies and power dynamics
3. Students' identities, positionality, and agency
4. Community partnerships
5. Balancing standardization with the particulars of a given context
6. Combining a battery of assessment types (qualitative and quantitative)
7. Cultural validity.

This suggested TSL assessment framework is the reconceptualization of critical language assessment within civic engagement and community partnerships that specifically emphasize the unique demands of applied ESL instruction. Avineri and Perren's (2019) work is grounded by both critical theory and critical pedagogy that prioritize the combined language and culture needs of students. Both critical reflection and critical-thinking processes are necessary for students to transform their volunteer community-service experiences into deeper understandings of course content.

Our Experiences Assessing Students in Service-Learning Courses

We have both been involved in TSL teams in Michigan, Pennsylvania, Florida, and California that included instructors, student assistants, program coordinators, and various administrative offices at different campus locations. The curriculum at each institution has focused on ESL program learning outcomes such as SL and language learning.

The CP sites visited were those focused on hunger, homelessness, and other topics. They included day care centers for children, food banks, food distribution centers, organizations serving homeless populations, affordable housing programs, city park departments, senior centers, K–12 sites for reading buddies, urban farming initiatives, regional environmental protection agencies, and neonatal care support organizations. The courses often involved delicate and sensitive social issues, necessitating a range of socially situated activities, assignments, and assessments that concentrated on the course learning outcomes. The distinct elements of the course we taught were coordinated with our established community partnerships and align with Feature 4.

The assignments we have used include pre-departure discussions, reading and writing assignments, reflection tasks, reading responses, role-play activities, vocabulary quizzes, and individual and group presentations. When appraised as a group of assessments, they provide an overall illustration of student language proficiency progress. Our viewpoint on utilizing a battery of assessment measures coincides with Feature 6.

Ongoing reflections during course segments allow students to experience course content from the perspective of an active participant (e.g., social entitlement, socioeconomic differences, etc.) by offering them opportunities to directly contextualize language learning and SL goals in real time through authentic communicative situations and problem solving. We used role-play activities to rehearse instruction giving-and-receiving scenarios and social exchanges of interactions at CP sites, presenting students with opportunities to verify language progress (Perren, 2008). Multiple discussion and reading responses, vocabulary tests, and individual and group presentations (formal and traditional assessment) delivered key formative and summative assessment information about distinct learning goals. These assignments provided students with multiple opportunities for recognition of relevant social issues and correspond with Feature 2, ideologies, and power dynamics.

Through these SL courses in ESL programs, our students have had many opportunities to explore abundant and relevant social issues and topics in the United States. ESL and EFL students were able to use language by communicating extensively on social challenges through interpersonal interactions (see Feature 1). Likewise, students engaged in numerous interactions alongside community members and CP representatives. You can similarly use this model to teach your ESL students how to use language for analysis of U.S. social issues, so they can be involved in finding solutions.

Exploration: ESL Exit Ticket for Community-Based Service-Learning

Using an exit ticket can be a regular class activity; with and without a CP visit, your students will learn routines for quick, on-their-feet recollection of learning. Preparing for future volunteer service situations is another focus of this distinct assessment concept. Follow these steps to determine what students have learned in some aspect of SL. Cell phones can be used.

1. Provide an example of an exit ticket. Tickets should include a space for the student's name and several questions (see Figure 4.1). Sample questions include: *What did you learn from today's lesson? What questions do you still have after this class?*

Name: _____	Name: _____
Date: _____	Date: _____
CP Site and Cause _____	Language Focus _____
How can you connect today's lesson to the real world?	[Insert your exit ticket question or direction here]

Figure 4.1 Sample Exit Tickets
Note: Courtesy of Microsoft Office Templates for education.

2. Explain the importance of a good exit-ticket response and format (e.g., ask students to respond by writing only two or three sentences).
3. Provide a sample exit ticket based on the type of question prompt you provide.
   a. The prompt (or question) can be a subset of a larger question set from the written reflection questions regularly used in your SL course for formative or summative assessment.
4. Decide on what content or combinations of content you would like to probe.
   a. The content can be language focused (grammar, pronunciation, vocabulary) or SL content focused (community partner service, social justice topic, personal development, etc.).
5. Decide (or ask students to decide) if the exit tickets should be graded.
6. Prepare your tickets by pre-printing them with your prompt.
   a. Type the prompt/question four times in a table with two columns and two rows, print it out, and then cut 8½ x 11 paper into four squares. This smaller size is helpful for limiting word count and for easy physical exchange of the exit tickets between you and the students.

7. Distribute the exit tickets approximately 10 minutes before the end of class to draw students' attention to the task.
   a. Inform students that they have two or three minutes to complete the exit ticket.
8. Collect the exit tickets from students as they leave the class or before class is dismissed, and then either read them as an activity then or later (a variation can be to have students read them and discuss; this depends on students' age and grade levels as well as their proficiency).
9. Alternatively, consider using an engaging assessment app, such as Quizlet or Kahoot or a dynamic learning website such as www.near pod.com for the entire exit-ticket process. Students can use their cell phones for all of these technology options.

The responses from the exit ticket will allow an ESL teacher incorporating SL to quickly understand more about the targeted TSL experience or academic content, and the information can be helpful in planning for the next class session.

Exploration: Socially Situated Language-in-Use Assessment of ESL Student Reading

In this activity, students improve their reading fluency and comprehension. Enhance students' reading comprehension with one reading strategy during a pre-departure reading activity about a SL social issue concerning a food drive before a national holiday, such as Thanksgiving. Follow these steps to determine what students have learned about the food drive reading and discussion topic related to the planned volunteer service of gathering the items in one's campus or community for the community partner.

1. Explain the related language learning objective for the service activity:
   a. At the end of this lesson, students will be able to determine meanings of new vocabulary through contextual clues.
2. Model how to guess the meaning of vocabulary from context as one reading strategy (e.g., ieltsbuddy.com/guessing-meaning-from-context.html).

3. Highlight several key vocabulary items from the article (e.g., about food drives) without their definitions.
4. Provide students with a sample reading material about the benefits of food drives, for example, for the community (e.g., washingtontimes. com/news/2019/dec/26/three-cheers-for-civil-and-charitable-society-this/).
5. Present this example from the article in step number 4 for students to practice:
   a. *It had been raining hard through the night, so the ground was saturated.*
   b. Ask *What does the word* saturated *mean?*
6. Discuss this reading (learning) strategy with students by stating something along these lines:
   a. "You may already know, but if you do not, you should be able to have a good guess from the rest of the sentence."
   b. "It had been raining, which means the ground must be wet. It was raining *hard* so this means the ground is probably very wet. *saturated = completely wet.*"
7. Ask students to practice with the reading materials and vocabulary provided, and work in pairs on the meanings of the highlighted vocabulary.

5. Making It Meaningful

Now that methods for creating, maintaining, and assessing your SL-focused class have been presented, it's time to dig a bit deeper and share useful discoveries we have made (through extensive trial and error), to make the experience more meaningful for students. While teaching a TSL class, we have found it frustrating to hear a student say that they didn't see how what they were doing in the course was helpful for their future. What made the comment even more discouraging was seeing all the skills the student was learning (small talk, email and thank-you letter writing, question-asking skills to name a few) and knowing that the experience would be immediately beneficial to this particular student's career goals. Nonetheless, the overwhelming majority of TSL research shows students making favorable comments about volunteering and its connection to their employment future, although there are some comments that show the opposite. After hearing similar critical comments from ESL students, we realized the importance of clearly communicating to students what is possible to gain from this type of course. Therefore, ideas about (1) connecting service activities and student career goals, (2) connecting with the campus community, and (3) standardizing of service-learning courses in TESOL are discussed next.

Connecting Service Activities to Student Career Goals

Students may come to your classes with an array of personal and professional experiences and career goals. Learning about your students' backgrounds and professional goals will help you start a course that will have a deeper meaning for them. On the first day of class, or even before the first day if you have access to student contact information, distribute a questionnaire that will help you learn about your students (see Figure 5.1). Individualizing the course to make it meet your students' needs will naturally make the course more meaningful.

Before asking students to fill out the survey, have a discussion about their fields of study, the careers they envision for themselves in the future, and the types of work skills (communicative, flexibility, teamwork, etc.) they want

Name:

Field of Study:

For a few minutes, reflect on and then write the skills needed for your future profession:

For a few minutes, reflect on and then write the skills that you currently have that could be helpful for service work:

What skills are you interested in working to improve?

Figure 5.1 Sample Questions on a Service-Learning Course Survey

to develop. Some students may not have thought explicitly about the skills they will need to make themselves marketable for the job that they want; this mindful and reflective process will help them do so.

The survey responses require students to think more deeply about what they can offer community partners in service activities and what they can get out of these activities as well. Asking students specifically about the types of skills they need for their future will force them to think carefully about what they are doing currently to hone those skills. After reviewing completed surveys, present the listed skills to the students and refer to them often when describing the SL activities you have organized. Ask students to refer to these skills in the reflection portion of the course so they clearly understand that they are not only being good community members but also gaining valuable career skills.

The information revealed from the survey responses will not only be beneficial on a personal-growth level but also for resume-building. In some circumstances, students are unable to obtain valuable work experience because of visa restrictions. Volunteer work can be a powerful way to acquire skills that will help them in their future careers, without violating visa restrictions. Note, however, that the U.S. Customs and Immigration and U.S. Department of Labor have specifications for what is permitted as volunteer work or employment (internationalcenter.umich.edu/students/employment-volunteer). It is not possible, for example, to do work that is not typically considered "volunteer work," or to complete activities that students could be paid for in the future. Before encouraging students to complete volunteer activities as potential job experience, be sure that both you and the student understand the government regulations.

Educators need to have learners see stronger and clearer connections between their career/professional skills and course materials and assignments (Frost et al., 2014). This makes sense, since many ESL students may express enthusiasm for earning high marks in lieu of seeking and discovering significant meaning, relating to ideas, and engaging with learning material directed by intrinsic curiosity and interest. "Strategic" learning is trying to get a grade and the latter is considered "deep" learning (Frost et al., 2014, p. 46). For learners to reach this level of deep learning, the focus of education should be on learning itself and is best guided by having ESL students understand language concepts through SL in real-life situations, such as those related to their chosen career choices. Perhaps with this notion incorporated into TSL, ESL students would demonstrate increased responsibility for their community experiences.

Connecting with the Campus Community

International students and ESL students often experience a disconnectedness from the community in which they live (Barratt & Huba, 1994; Charles & Stewart, 1991; Yeh & Inose, 2003). Providing ESL students with opportunities to become active in the university or academic institution community can alleviate some of these problems. The community of the English language classroom tends to be a very safe and comforting place for international or ESL students, even though this space is not permanent. To foster a feeling of comfort and connectedness, it is important to find ways to incorporate community-wide interaction in the classroom.

Depending on your teaching circumstances, you may be able to promote your SL course and activities more broadly on campus. Most universities and K–12 settings have a news site (or school newspaper) to share current happenings across campus. Consider contacting the news editors and ask them to write about the work that your international or ESL students are doing. This is not only a positive promotion of the class itself but also an acknowledgment of the role that the international and ESL students play on your campus. When students see this information published in the school news, they will feel a sense of pride and see a clear meaning in the SL activities that they have completed. The same sentiment applies to a department or school Facebook page or website. Including a picture and story of the SL activities on social media informs everyone on the great work that is happening in your ESL classroom. These easily sharable articles show that students are a valuable part of the department, school, and community.

In addition to making students feel like they are part of the community, ESL teachers should try to bridge the potential gap between domestic students and international or ESL students. To do this, consider opening up your SL activities to domestic students. This creates valuable learning opportunities for both parties. Studies have shown that international students have increased contentment and satisfaction when they have a higher ratio of friendships with locals (Hendrickson et al., 2011), but the ability to have these friendships is very much linked to students' speaking proficiency (Kudo & Simkin, 2003). To build up ESL students' speaking confidence, they must have opportunities to practice in realistic circumstances. One option for this connection in the K–12 setting is to create a buddy-like system where ESL and non-ESL students complete the SL activity together. At the university level, an example is for students in global-focused or international language fields to join the SL experience with ESL or international students. These options produce an incredibly meaningful experience for all involved. Both resume-building and character-building opportunities transpire when groups are brought together.

Standardizing Service-Learning in TESOL

In the 1980s, education reform in the United States was driven by the establishment of academic standards that described the academic information and content students should know and be able to do. At that time, national and state standards were used to guide other educational system components (e.g., in the field of teacher education). The standards-based education reform movement initially represented the need for measurable and coherent academic standards for school students (Glavin, 2014). Since that time, educational standards reform has influenced assessment and testing. Most readers are undoubtedly aware of the past and present debates about the advantages and disadvantages of the educational standardization process (see Bennett, 2019; Bjerede, 2013; Lefkowits & Miller, 2006; Sarapini & Callejo Perez, 2015). Needless to say, the TESOL field has also been affected by this movement. However, "even though a curriculum may be standard, teachers need to use a variety of teaching approaches to meet the needs of diverse student populations" (Sarapini & Callejo Perez, 2015, p. 1).

In response to the standardization movement, ten principles regarding service-learning were introduced by Honnet and Poulsen (1989). The items in this model were originally enacted as a "good service-learning practices" and are listed here:

Principles for Combining Service and Learning

1. An effective program engages people in responsible and challenging actions for the common good.
2. An effective program provides structured opportunities for people to reflect critically on their service experience.
3. An effective program articulates clear service and learning goals for everyone involved.
4. An effective program allows for those with needs to define those needs.
5. An effective program clarifies the responsibilities of each person and organization involved.
6. An effective program matches service providers and service needs through a process that recognizes changing circumstances.
7. An effective program expects genuine, active, and sustained organizational commitment.
8. An effective program includes training, supervision, monitoring, support, recognition, and evaluation to meet service and learning goals.
9. An effective program ensures that the time commitment for service and learning is flexible, appropriate, and in the best interests of all involved.
10. An effective program is committed to program participation by and with diverse populations.

The principles approach to SL allows for clear direction for effective instruction in many service-learning contexts as it was originally intended. This is opposed to planning and initiating a service-learning course in a haphazard manner. It clarifies how a teacher can prepare for beneficial student learning by following these ten principles. As useful as this model might be, there is an important gap—there is no specific information for connecting language and culture related issues to L2 learners. The primary language and culture-focused components are often outlined in various TESOL educational standards for practice, but they are not included in Honnet and Poulsen's (1989) principles for good SL practices model. Prioritizing language and culture is an important step to take toward the maturation of a standardized pedagogical practice for community engagement through English as a second language education. This approach would better meet the needs of ESL/EFL students as well as teacher education programs.

This could possibly include providing a framework for integrating paired learning objectives for each lesson or specific sub-section of a lesson modeled on what has been accomplished with the Sheltered Instruction Observation Protocol (SIOP) (Echevarria et al., 2017). The SIOP Model emphasizes lesson and syllabus development, instructional practices, and assessment by linking language-related objectives with content-related objectives from four areas: math, science, social studies, and language arts. We propose a similar process in TESOL Service-Learning (TSL) by combining a language content learning objective and a social justice content learning objective, to be included in each activity, lesson, syllabus, and program because this allows for balance between the two content areas of social justice/civic engagement on the one hand, and critical language related elements on the other. New standardization features should be commenced and implemented in a systematic manner.

Final Thoughts

The concept of TSL has gained momentum as an alternative to classroom learning. We hope we have guided you, the ESL teacher, with some of the information that we have gained with a combined 30 years of teaching and research on this topic. We also hope you have learned more about critical thinking and reflection in both written and oral forms that you can use for students to deepen their course content knowledge whether from the four skills, grammar, and vocabulary, or important social justice and civic engagement topics relevant to your community context. A course structure of this type will allow for stronger connections between the service they provide, their learning, and achievement of learning outcomes.

SL can add to traditional ESL classroom learning by allowing learners to benefit from the service they provide to the community, the people they interact with, and the reflections they discuss and write. TSL is a high-impact practice and a transformative pedagogy that includes critical reflection of student experiences as well as opportunities for students to act as both teachers and learners. We believe we have illustrated many of the personal and social benefits of ESL students' being engaged in service learning—particularly, experiencing a sense of belonging in the community, gaining a sense of empowerment, and becoming more critically aware of social issues. In addition, we have shown evidence of how pre-service teachers have demonstrated personal, academic, and professional growth.

Another goal was to show how SL projects can create opportunities for ESL students to explore educational programs by using authentic communication and add to valuable hands-on practice for their professional goals. We hope that the material in this ebook has provided you with a starting point for using SL in your ESL courses and will expand your teaching repertoire by doing so. By exploring your ability to integrate SL pedagogy in your ESL teaching, you will also contribute further to the common good, one of the primary conceptual and practical origins of this pedagogical approach.

Appendix A
Sample Syllabus for an ESL Service-Learning Course

Course Description: This course provides students with practice in the English listening/speaking skills necessary to succeed in the American university. It also will provide students with the chance to combine critical thinking with practical experience as they make an active contribution with community-based projects. Students will learn about themselves and their community.

Course Objectives:

- Enhance critical thinking and interpersonal skills
- Develop a better understanding of course content
- Advance academic performance and retention
- Promote learning through active participation
- Provide structured time for students to reflect
- Supply opportunities to use skills and knowledge in real-life situations
- Extend learning beyond the classroom
- Foster a sense of caring for others

Students will be able to:

1. Participate in hands-on experiential active learning in listening/speaking situations outside the classroom;
2. Engage in responsible and challenging actions for the common good;
3. Reflect critically on the service experience;
4. Keep regular and detailed online and audio journal entries on Instagram that include reflections, observations, thoughts, and feelings about the community events and the service experiences;
5. Use those journal entries as the basis for an final oral presentation using Microsoft PowerPoint software.

Course format: Exercises and activities for practicing language skills are taken from authentic language (vocabulary, idiom and phrasal verbs) found in on-site locations in the local area. These sites are where students will be interacting and engaging in voluntary community service. Classroom lectures will be another important source of authentic language. Listening, speaking, and reading and writing skills will be facilitated by a myriad of activities which include:

- group discussions based on questions about vocabulary, main ideas, and supporting details in reading materials/lectures;
- group discussions based on what community service means to each student;
- group discussions based on plans for each community service project;
- group discussions based on an on-going assessment of each service project;
- communication resulting from interaction between students/ supervisors/clients;
- end-of-the term oral presentation based on each student's community service.

Time Commitment: Students will spend approximately 15–20 hours during the semester at sites in the local area performing various acts of community-based service. The remaining hours will be spent on campus in the in the classroom.

Grade Information:

Attendance and Participation	15%
Reflection Writings	20%
Formal Assessments	30%
Oral Presentation	15%
ESL Day of Service Project	10%
Various Homework	10%

Attendance and Participation 15%:
Students taking this course are required to attend all class sessions and actively participate in the extensive group discussions. Additionally, an attendance sheet will be maintained to record the hours completing service at the community partner site.

Reflection Writings 20%:

Students are to maintain a self-reflective journal for each service session. Students will be provided questions to evoke their thinking during the service. Students will also receive an example reflection for reference.

Formal Assessments (quizzes, midterm, final exam) 30%:

Quizzes will be given on a weekly basis. Questions are from the reading materials covered in class. Exams cover questions from the quizzes but may include additional reading, listening, and writing tasks.

Oral Presentation 15%:

At the end of the term, students will give a five-minute oral report summarizing their community service experience. Successes and problems during the service will be outlined and discussed.

ESL Day of Service Project 10%:

We will plan an ESL Day of Service in which all students and faculty in the department will be invited to volunteer with our class. Throughout the semester, we will work together to 1) choose a community partner to work with, 2) inform and invite others to join (creating flyers, writing informational emails, and visiting classes), and 3) communicate with the community partner to plan the day.

Everyone will be given a role to facilitate planning this ESL Day of Service. (see assignments).

Various Homework 10%:

Various homework including reading, writing, listening, vocabulary will be assigned.

Appendix B
TESOL Service-Learning Assignments and Activities

1. ESL Day of Service Assignment

This semester, you will be in charge of teaching and organizing a class outing. You are in charge of every aspect of it.

Name	Date of Event	Event
		Examples

Guidelines:

1. Decide the logistics:
   When will we go? Choose date and time. Have a backup plan in case of bad weather.
   How will we get there?
   How much does it cost? Should we bring cash with us?
   What are the rules we need to know before we go?
   What should we wear?
2. Meet with me to discuss the logistics at least one week before the trip.
3. Teach the class about your field trip at least two days before we go:

You must provide:

- 3–5 minutes presentation
- A PowerPoint type slide show (Google Slides, PPT, or Prezi)
- Use at least two vocabulary words from what we've studied by the time you present.
- Teach us at least two words/phrases about the place you will be leading us to.
- A copy of your lesson plan, using the template below as a guide (bring this to your meeting with me so that you can receive some feedback before you present).

Lesson plan template (guide only...feel free to change as necessary!)

Amount of Time	Activity	Materials Needed
30 seconds– 1 minute	Greetings, introductions	PPT slides
1–2 minutes	Background information of event (5Ws)	
2–3 minutes	Logistics of participating in event	
3–5 minutes	Q&A, conclusion	

2. Humans of _____ Assignment

Your task is to interview someone involved in a community partner site. You will model this on the Humans of New York Instagram structure. This means you will interview someone, write their story, and use presentation software to visually tell their story. Your interviewee must:

- Ask their permission to interview them. If they are willing, take a picture or two of them to include in your project. You may ask them any questions you'd like, but the goal is to tell their life story (past or present) in your presentation. You will present your work in class.

3. Community Research Project

This group project is to give you an opportunity to find out more about some part of life in the United States or American culture. The focus should be on aspects related to the services or missions of our community partner sites. Some examples:

- How many people go to bed hungry in our county?
- Where do food banks get food from?
- How is food dispersed from food banks?

There are multiple parts to this project:

1. **Choose** a topic.
2. **Research** the topic online.
3. **Make a plan** to ask questions (in person or phone call—with your partner).

4. **Interview** someone from a community partner and ask your questions.

5. **Create** a presentation with your group members to talk about what you learned.

6. **Take** pictures or find pictures online to add to the presentation.

You will contact local people to research for this project. You can go to a place and talk to people, make a phone call, research online... but you MUST speak to someone (phone or in-person.) You can ask short questions on the phone or meet someone in person and have a longer interview.

4. Sample Activities

(1) *The ESL Day of Service Assignment* (short description): This semester, you will be in charge of teaching and organizing a class outing. You are in charge of every aspect of it.

(2) *Humans of An Example City/Town Assignment* (short description): Your task is to interview someone involved in a community partner site. You will model this on the Humans of New York Instagram structure. This means you will interview someone, write their story, and use presentation software to visually tell their story.

(3) *The Community Research Project* (short description): This group project is to give you an opportunity to find out more about some part of life in the United States or American culture. The focus should be on aspects related to the services or missions of our community partner sites.

Appendix C
TESOL Service-Learning Resources

Service-Learning Research Resources

- Journal of Service Learning in Higher Education:
  https://journals.sfu.ca/jslhe/index.php/jslhe
- National Center for Service-Learning:
  https://www.nationalservice.gov/resources/service-learning
- Michigan Journal of Service-Learning: https://ginsberg.umich.edu/
  mijournal

Virtual Teaching Resources

- California State University/Long Beach:
  http://www.csulb.edu/center-for-community-engagement
- There is up-to-date Covid-19 information currently available on this
  website as well as a link to YouTube videos about CSULB's useful
  resources in post-pandemic era.
- Association of College and University Educators Online teaching
  toolkit (2020):
  https://acue.org/online-teaching-toolkit/

Service-Learning Assessment Resources

- Carleton University Service-Learning Assessment Resources: https://
  serc.carleton.edu/NAGTWorkshops/servicelearning/assessment.html
- Center for Advanced Research on Language Acquisition, University of
  Minnesota:
  http://www.carla.umn.edu/assessment/resources.html

- DePaul University:
  https://resources.depaul.edu/teaching-commons/teaching-guides/
  feedback-grading/Pages/assessing-reflection.aspx
- San Francisco State University: Center for Civic and Community
  Engagement: https://icce.sfsu.edu/content/assessing-service-learning

BIBLIOGRAPHY

Ash, S., & Clayton, P. (2009). Generating, deepening, and documenting learning. *Journal of Applied Learning in Higher Education, 1,* 25–28.

Askildson, L. R., Kelly, A. C., & Mick, C. S. (2013). Developing multiple literacies in academic English through service-learning and community engagement. *TESOL Journal, 4*(3), 402–438.

Avineri, N. (2015). Nested interculturality, multiple knowledges, and situated identities through service-learning in language education. In J. M. Perren & A. J. Wurr (Eds.), *Learning the language of global citizenship: Strengthening service-learning in TESOL* (pp. 197–223). Champaign, IL: Common Ground Publishers.

Avineri, N., & Perren, J. (2019). Language testing in service-learning: A critical approach to socially-situated language-in-use. In M. Seyed Abdolhamid & P. I. De Costa (Eds.), *Sociopolitics of language testing.* New York: Bloomsbury Publishing.

Bandi, J. (2020). *What is service learning or civic engagement?* Nashville, TN: Vanderbilt University Center for Teaching. Retrieved from https://cft.vanderbilt.edu/guides-sub-pages/teaching-through-community-engagement/

Bardovi-Harlig, K., & Mahan-Taylor, R. (2003). *Teaching pragmatics.* Washington, DC: U.S. Department of State.

Barratt, M. F., & Huba, M. E. (1994). Factors related to international undergraduate student adjustment in an American community. *College Student Journal, 28,* 422–435.

Be My Eyes (2020). Bringing sight to blind and low-vision people. Retrieved from http://www.bemyeyes.com

Bennett, C. (2019, January 30). Choice motivates students when rewards and punishment don't work. Retrieved from https://www.thoughtco.com/when-rewards-and-punishment-dont-work-3996919

Bickel, B., Shin, J. K., Taylor, J., Faust, H., & Penniston, T. (2013). Learning English internationally while engaging communities locally: Online EFL supporting community learning for young leaders. *TESOL Journal, 4*(3), 439–462.

Billig, S. H., & Eyler, J. (2003). The state of service-learning and service-learning research. In S. H. Billig & J. Eyler (Eds.), *Deconstructing service-learning: Research exploring context, participation, and impacts* (pp. 253–264). Greenwich, CT: Information Age.

Bippus, S. L., & Eslami, Z. R. (2013). Adult ESOL students and service-learning: Voices, experiences, and perspectives. *TESOL Journal, 4*(3), 587–597.

Bjerede, M. (2013, April 26). Education standardization: Essential or harmful? *Getting Smart.* Retrieved from https://www.gettingsmart.com/2013/04/education-standardization-essential-or-harmful/

Breen, M. P., & Littlejohn, A. (2000). *Classroom decision-making: Negotiation and process syllabuses in practice.* Cambridge, UK: Cambridge University Press.

Brennan, C. J. (2009). Realizing the benefits of computer assisted language learning (CALL) in English language learning classrooms. *Interfaces, 3*(1), 1–28.

Bringle, R. G. (2003). Enhancing theory-based learning in service-learning. In S. H. Billig & J. Eyler (Eds.), *Deconstructing service-learning: Research exploring context, participation, and impacts* (pp. 3–21). Greenwich, CT: Information Age.

Bringle, R. G., Hatcher, J. A., & Jones, S. G. (Eds.). (2011). *International service learning: Conceptual frameworks and research.* Sterling, VA: Stylus.

California State University Center of Community Engagement (2010). Best practices for managing risk in service-learning. Retrieved from https://www.calstate.edu/cce/resource_center/documents/archive/Final_BestPracticesManual-02.pdf

California State University Northridge Community Engagement (2020). California State University—Northridge community engagement. Retrieved from https://www.csun.edu/undergraduate-studies/community-engagement

Cameron, L. M. (2015). Attitude, behaviors, and the longitudinal impact of social justice service-learning for language learners. In J. M. Perren & A. J. Wurr (Eds.), *Learning the language of global citizenship: Strengthening service-learning in TESOL* (pp. 56–79). Champaign, IL: Common Ground.

Cardellio, K. (2016). Situated directives in Italian L2 service-learning encounters. Unpublished doctoral diss., University of South Florida, Tampa.

Celce-Murcia, M., Brinton, D. M., & Snow, M. A. (Eds.). (2014). *Teaching English as a second or foreign language.* Boston, MA: Cengage Learning.

Charles, H., & Stewart, M. (1991). Academic advising of international students. *Journal of Multicultural Counseling and Development, 19,* 173–180.

Clayton, P. (n.d.). The DEAL model for critical reflection—Describe, examine, and articulate learning. Retrieved from http://servicelearning.duke.edu/

Community Engagement. (2020). *Types of service-learning.* Cedar Falls: University of Northern Iowa Community Engagement. Retrieved from https://engagement.uni.edu/service-learning/course-designation/types-service-learning

Cooney, E. (2015). Island to island: TESOL students teach homeless Micronesian migrants in Hawaiʻi. In J. M. Perren & A. J. Wurr (Eds.), *Learning the language of global citizenship: Strengthening service-learning in TESOL* (pp. 396–427). Champaign, IL: Common Ground.

Coxhead, A. (Ed.). (2014). *New ways in teaching vocabulary.* Alexandria, VA: TESOL Press.

Christensson, P. (2011, December 21). *Web publishing definition.* Minneapolis, MN: Tech Terms. Retrieved from https://techterms.com/definition/web_publishing

Crossman, J. M., & Kite, S. L. (2007). Their perspectives: ESL students' reflections on collaborative community service learning. *Business Communication Quarterly, 70*(2), 147–165. doi: 10.1177/1080569907301776

DeGregoriis, J. (2006). *Literacy and the ELL student: Best practices for increasing reading development.* Alexandria, VA: TESOL. Retrieved from https://www.tesol.org/docs/default-source/new-resource-library/literacy-and-the-ell-student-a-literature-review.pdf?sfvrsn=0&sfvrsn=0

Dewey, J. (1938). *Education and experience.* New York: Macmillan.

Duguid, F., Mündel, K., & Schugurensky, D. (2013). *Volunteer work, informal learning and social action.* Rotterdam, The Netherlands: Sense Publishers.

Echevarria, J., Vogt, M., & Short, D. (2017). *Making content comprehensible for English language learners: The SIOP Model.* London: Pearson Publishers.

Ediger, A. (2014). Teaching second/foreign language literacy to school-age learners. In M. Celce-Murcia, M. A. Snow, & D. Brinton (Eds.), *Teaching English as a second or foreign language* (4th ed., pp. 154–169). Boston, MA: National Geographic/Cengage Learning.

Ene, E., & Orlando, H. (2015). Integrating service-learning in EAP programs: Building the village that it takes. In J. M. Perren & A. J. Wurr (Eds.), *Learning the language of global citizenship: Strengthening service-learning in TESOL* (pp. 112–139). Champaign, IL: Common Ground.

Engaging by Communicating (n.d.). *Communication strategies for service learning.* Greenville, NC: East Carolina University. Retrieved from http://core.ecu.edu/dumlaor/strategies.html

Eyler, J., & Giles, D. E. (1999). *Where's the learning in service learning?* San Francisco, CA: Jossey-Bass.

Ferris, D., & Hedgcock, J. S. (2004). *Teaching ESL composition: Purpose, process, and practice.* London: Routledge.

Fioramonte, A. (2014). A study of pragmatic competence: International medical graduates' and patients' negotiation of treatment phase of medical encounters. Unpublished doctoral diss., University of South Florida, Tampa.

Fitzgerald, C. M. (2009). Language and community: Using service learning to recon figure the multicultural classroom. *Language and Education, 23*(3), 217–231. DOI:10.1080/09500780802510159

Frost, G., Connolly, M., & Lapanno, E. (2014). Why is it so hard to do a good thing? The challenges of using reflection to help sustain a commitment to learning. *Collected Essays on Learning and Teaching, 7*(1), 46–49.

Furco, A. (1996). Service-learning: A balanced approach to experiential education. In Taylor, B. and Corporation for National Service (Eds.), *Expanding boundaries: Service and learning* (pp. 2–6). Washington, DC: Corporation for National Service.

Graves, K. (2014). Syllabus and curriculum design for second language teaching. In M. Celce-Murcia, M. A. Snow, & D. Brinton (Eds.), *Teaching English as a second or foreign language* (4th ed., pp. 46–62). Boston, MA: National Geographic/Cengage Learning.

Gelmon, S. B., Holland, B. A., Driscoll, A., Spring, A., & Kerrigan, S. (2001). *Assessing service-learning and civic engagement: Principles and techniques.* Providence, RI: Campus Compact.

Giles, D. E., & Eyler, J. (1994). The theoretical roots of service-learning in John Dewey: Toward a theory of service learning. *Michigan Journal of Community Service Learning, 1*(1), 77–85.

Glavin, C. (2014). Standards-based education reform: K–12 academics. Retrieved from https://www.k12academics.com/education-reform/standards-based-education-reform

Glicker, E. (2006). Service-learning for academic literacy in adult ESL programs. *The CATESOL Journal, 18*(1), 40–47.

Goh, C. C. M. (2014). Second language listening comprehension: Process and pedagogy. In M. Celce-Murcia, M. A. Snow, & D. Brinton (Eds.), *Teaching English as a second or foreign language* (4th ed., pp. 72–89). Boston, MA: National Geographic/Cengage Learning.

Guillén, G., Sawin, T., & Avineri, N. (2020). Zooming out of the
crisis: Language and human collaboration. *Foreign Language Annals*, 1–9.

Hafernik, J. J., Messerschmitt, D. S., & Vandrick, S. (2002). *Ethical issues for
ESL faculty: Social justice in practice.* Mahwah, NJ: Lawrence Erlbaum.

Hagar, T. (2019). Practical applications of TESOL's "The 6 principles
for exemplary teaching of English learners." *English Teaching Forum,*
57(1), 44–52.

Harmer, J. (2007). *The practice of English language teaching* (4th ed.). Harlow,
UK: Pearson Longman.

Healey, D., Hanson-Smith, E., Hubbard, P., Ioannou-Georgiou, S., Kessler,
G., & Ware, P. (2011). *TESOL technology standards framework.* Alexandria,
VA: TESOL.

Hemphill, B. (2015). *Social justice as a moral imperative. The Open Journal of
Occupational Therapy, 3*(2), 1–9.

Hendrickson, B., Rosen, D., & Aune, R. K. (2011). An analysis of friendship
networks, social connectedness, homesickness, and satisfaction levels
of international students. *International Journal of Intercultural Relations,*
35(3), 281–295. DOI:10.1016/j.ijintrel.2010.08.001

Hinkel, E. (2014). Culture and pragmatics in language teaching and learning.
In M. Celce-Murcia, M. A. Snow, & D. Brinton (Eds.), *Teaching English as
a second or foreign language* (4th ed., pp. 394–408). Boston, MA: National
Geographic/Cengage Learning.

Homes, J. (2000). Talking English from 9 to 5: Challenges for ESL learners at
work. *International Journal of Applied Linguistics, 10*(1), 125–140.

Honnet, E. P., & Poulsen, S. J. (1989). *Wingspread special report: Principles of
good practice for combining service and learning.* Racine, WI: The Johnson
Foundation.

Howard, J. (Ed.). (2001). *Service-learning course design workbook.* Ann Arbor,
MI: OCSL Press.

Hummel, K. M. (2013). Target language community involvement: Second
language linguistic self-confidence and other perceived benefits. *The
Canadian Modern Language Review/ La Revue canadienne des langues
vivantes, 69*(1), 65–90. doi:10.3138/cmlr.1152

Jacoby, B. (2003). Fundamentals of service-learning partnerships. In B.
Jacoby (Ed.), *Building partnerships for service-learning* (pp. 1–19). San
Francisco, CA: John Wiley & Sons.

Karasik, R. J. (2013). Reflecting on reflection: Capitalizing on the learning in
intergenerational service-learning. *Gerontology & Geriatrics Education,*
34(1), 78–98. DOI: 10.1080/02701960.2013.749252

Katz, A. (2014). Assessment in second language classrooms. In M. Celce-Murcia, D. M. Brinton, & M. A. Snow (Eds.), *Teaching English as a second or foreign language* (pp. 320–337). Boston, MA: National Geographic/Cengage Learning.

Khan, H. (2017, March 9). The importance of speaking in second language acquisition. *ESL Article*. Retrieved from http://eslarticle.com/pub/english-as-a-second-language-esl/139477-The-Importance-of-Speaking-in-Second-Language-Acquisition.html

Kim, Y., & Taguchi, N. (2016). Learner-learner interaction during collaborative pragmatic tasks: The role of cognitive and pragmatic task demands. *Foreign Language Annals, 49*(1), 42–57.

Kincaid, N. M., & Sotiriou, P. (2004). Service learning at an urban two-year college. *Teaching English in the Two-Year College, 31*(3), 248–259.

Kisslinger, E. (2000). *J-Talk: Conversation across cultures.* Oxford, UK: Oxford University Press.

Kolb, D. A. (1984). *Experiential learning: Experience as the source of learning and development.* Englewood Cliffs, NJ: Prentice-Hall.

Kudo, K., & Simkin, K. A. (2003). Intercultural friendship formation: The case of Japanese students at an Australian university. *Journal of Intercultural Studies, 24*(2), 91–114.

Kuh, G. D. (2008). *High-impact educational practices: What they are, who has access to them, and why they matter.* Washington, DC: Association of American Colleges and Universities.

Kumaravadivelu, B. (2006). *Understanding language teaching: From method to postmethod.*

Kurzweil, J., & Scholl, M. (2007). *Understanding teaching through learning.* New York: McGraw-Hill.

Lazaraton, A. (2014). Second language speaking. In M. Celce-Murcia, D. M. Brinton, & M. A. Snow (Eds), *Teaching English as a second or foreign language* (pp. 106–120). Boston, MA: National Geographic/Cengage Learning.

Learning to Give (2019). Literacy service-learning toolkit. Retrieved from https://www.learningtogive.org/resources/literacy-service-learning-toolkit

Lefkowits, L., & Miller, K. (2006). Fulfilling the promise of the standards movement. *Phi Delta Kappan, 87*(5), 403–407.

Leu, D., Kinzer, C., Coiro, J., & Cammack, D. (2004). Toward a theory of new literacies emerging from the internet and other information and communication technologies. In R. B. Ruddell & N. J. Unrau (Eds.), *Theoretical models and processes of reading* (5th ed., pp. 1570–1613). Newark, DE: International Reading Association.

Leung, C., & Lewkowicz, M. (2006). Expanding horizons and unresolved conundrums: Language testing and assessment. *TESOL Quarterly, 4*(1), 211–234.

Liu, F., Sulpizio S., Kornpetpanee, S., & Job, R. (2017). It takes biking to learn: Physical activity improves learning a second language. *PLoS ONE, 12*(5): e0177624. Retrieved from https://doi.org/10.1371/journal.pone.0177624

Long, M. (1996). The role of the linguistic environment in second language acquisition. In W. Ritchie & T. Bhatia (Eds.), *Handbook of second language acquisition* (pp. 413–468). San Diego, CA: Academic Press.

Louw, K., Derwing, T., & Abbot, M. (2010). Teaching pragmatics to L2 learners for the workplace: The job interview. *The Canadian Modern Language Review, 66*(5), 739–758.

Maloy, J., Comeau-Kirschner, C., & Amaral, J. (2015). Building a human rights curriculum to support digital service-learning. In J. M. Perren & A. J. Wurr (Eds.), *Learning the language of global citizenship: Strengthening service-learning in TESOL* (pp. 246–273). Champaign, IL: Common Ground.

Meier, J. (2015). When the experiential and multi-modal go global: Lessons from three community projects in a "Preparation for College Writing" class. In J. M. Perren & A. J. Wurr (Eds.), *Learning the language of global citizenship: Strengthening service-learning in TESOL* (pp. 140–168). Champaign, IL: Common Ground.

Messerschmitt, D. S., & Hafernik, J. J. (2009). *Dilemmas in teaching English to speakers of other languages: 40 cases.* Ann Arbor: The University of Michigan Press.

Mijares, L. (2007). The advantages of communicative language teaching. *The Internet TESL Journal, 13*(2). Retrieved from http://io.uvmnet.edu/revistadyn/app/articulo/ArticuloDyn.aspx?id=674

Miller, J., Berkey, B., & Griffin, F. (2015). International students in American pathway programs: Learning English and culture through service-learning. *Journal of International Students, 5*(4), 334–352. Retrieved from https://www.ojed.org/index.php/jis/article/view/399

Miller, J., & Kostka, I. (2015). Bridging cultures and generations: An exploration of intergenerational and intercultural oral history projects with English language learners. In J. M. Perren & A. J. Wurr (Eds.), *Learning the language of global citizenship: Strengthening service-learning in TESOL* (pp. 80–108). Champaign, IL: Common Ground.

Minor, J. L. (2002). Incorporating service learning into ESOL programs. *TESOL Journal, 11*(4), 10–14.

Molee, L. M., Henry, M. E., Sessa, V. I., & McKinney-Prupis, E. R. (2010). Assessing learning in service-learning courses through critical reflection. *The Journal of Experiential Education, 33*(3), 239–257. DOI:10.5193/JEE33.3.239

Nation, I. S. P. (2001). *Learning vocabulary in another language.* Cambridge, UK: Cambridge University Press.

Nation, I. S. P. (2009). *Teaching ESL/EFL reading and writing.* New York: Routledge.

National Service-Learning Clearinghouse (2011). Toolkit for the evaluation of service-learning programs. Retrieved from https://www.emich.edu> evaluation_assessment.pdf

National Service-Learning Clearinghouse (2020). Community wealth. Retrieved from https://community-wealth.org/content/national-service-learning-clearinghouse

Ni, P. (2014, November 16). How to communicate effectively with older adults. *Psychology Today.* Retrieved from https://www.psychologytoday.com/us/blog/communication-success/201411/how-communicate-effectively-older-adults

Overfield, D. M. (2007). Conceptualizing service learning as second language acquisition space: Directions for research. In A. J. Wurr & J. Hellebrandt (Eds.), *Learning the language of global citizenship: Service-learning in applied linguistics* (pp. 58–81). Bolton, MA: Anker.

Oxford, R. L., (1990). *Language learning strategies: What every teacher should know.* Boston, MA: Heinle & Heinle.

Perren, J. M. (2007). International service-learning in the Philippines: Community building through intercultural communication and second language use. In A.J. Wurr & J. Hellebrandt (Eds.), *Learning the language of global citizenship: Service-learning in Applied Linguistics* (pp. 263–292). Bolton, MA: Anker.

Perren, J. M. (2008). Intercultural language socialization through volunteering: A qualitative study of directive use in nonprofit organizations. Unpublished doctoral diss., Temple University, Philadelphia.

Perren, J. (2012, Nov. 1). Table Tents for TESOL. *TESOL Connections.*

Perren, J. M. (2013). Strategic steps to successful service-learning in TESOL: From critical to practical. *TESOL Journal, 4*(3), 487–513.

Perren, J. M., Grove, N., & Thornton, J. (2013). Three empowering curricular innovations for service-learning in ESL programs. *TESOL Journal, 4*(3), 463–486.

Perren, J. M., & Wurr, A. J. (Eds.). (2015). *Learning the language of global citizenship: Strengthening service-learning in TESOL*. Champaign, IL: Common Ground.

Pine, N. (2008). Service learning in a basic writing class: A best case scenario. *Journal of Basic Writing, 27*(2), 29–55.

Purgason, K. B. (2014). Lesson planning in second/foreign language teaching. In M. Celce-Murcia, M. A. Snow, & D. Brinton (Eds.), *Teaching English as a second or foreign language* (4th ed., pp. 362–379). Boston, MA: National Geographic/Cengage Learning.

Purmensky, K. L. (2009). *Service-learning for diverse communities: Critical pedagogy and mentoring English language learners*. Charlotte, NC: Information Age Publishing.

Purmensky, K. L. (2015). Bridging the gap for English learners: Service-learning digital mentorship for school success. In J. M. Perren & A. J. Wurr (Eds.), *Learning the language of global citizenship: Strengthening service-learning in TESOL* (pp. 569–598). Champaign, IL: Common Ground.

Rochford, R. A. (2013). Service-learning for remedial reading and writing students. *Community College Journal of Research and Practice, 37*(5), 345–355. DOI:10.1080/10668926.2010.532463

Roever, C. (2011). Testing of second language pragmatics: Past and future. *Language Testing, 28*(4), 463–481.

Roodin, P., Brown, L. H., & Shedlock, D. (2013). Intergenerational service-learning: A review of recent literature and directions for the future. *Gerontology & Geriatrics Education, 34*(1), 3–25. DOI:10.1080/02701960.2012.755624

Sarapini, E. F., & Callejo Perez, C. M. (2015). A perspective on the standardized curriculum and its effect on teaching and learning. *Journal of Education & Social Policy, 2*(5), 78–87.

Schmidt-Kassow, M., Kulka, A., Gunter, T. C., Rothermich, K., & Kotz, S. A. (2010). Exercising during learning improves vocabulary acquisition: Behavioral and ERP evidence. *Neuroscience Letters, 482*(1), 40–44. DOI: 10.1016/j.neulet.2010.06.089 Retrieved from https://digitalcommons.unomaha.edu/slcestgen/119

Schneider, J. (2019). Teaching in context: Integrating community-based service learning into TESOL education. *TESOL Journal, 10*(1), 1–15. Retrieved from https://doi.org/10.1002/tesj.380

Sigmon, R. L. (1979, Spring). Service-learning: Groping toward a definition. Experiential Education. *National Society for Experiential Education, 12*(1), 2–4.

Stanton, T. K., Giles, D. E., Jr., & Cruz, N. I. (1999). *Service-learning: A movement's pioneers reflect on its origins, practice, and future.* San Francisco, CA: Jossey-Bass.

Steinke, M. H. (2009). Learning English by helping others: Implementing service learning into the ESOL Classroom. *The Journal of Civic Commitment, 12*(Spring). Retrieved from http://www.mesacc.edu/other/engagement/Journal/index12.shtml

TESOL 2018. *The 6 principles for exemplary teaching of English learners: Grades K–12.* Alexandria, VA: TESOL.

U.S. Department of State (2015). The lighter side: Small talk. *English Teaching Forum, 53*(3). Retrieved from https://americanenglish.state.gov/resources/english-teaching-forum-2015-volume-53-number-3#child-1991

Verner, S. (n.d.). Four great grouping strategies for more effective ESL group work. *Fluent U.* Retrieved from https://www.fluentu.com/blog/educator-english/esl-group-work/

Vygotsky, L. S. (1978). *Mind in society: The development of higher psychological processes.* Cambridge, MA: Harvard University Press.

Wade, R. C. (2001). And justice for all: Community service-learning for social justice (Issue Paper). Denver, CO: Education Commission of the States.

Wagner, S., & Lopez, J. G. (2015). Meeting the challenges of service-learning teaching with international TESOL student teachers. In J. M. Perren & A. J. Wurr (Eds.), *Learning the language of global citizenship: Strengthening service-learning in TESOL* (pp. 277–305). Champaign, IL: Common Ground.

Warschauer, M. (1996). Motivational aspects of using computers for writing and Communication. In M. Warschauer (Ed.), Telecollaboration in foreign language learning: Proceedings of the Hawai'i symposium (Technical Report #12, pp. 29–46). Honolulu: University of Hawai'i, Second Language Teaching & Curriculum Center.

Warschauer, M., & Cook, J. (1999). Service learning and technology in TESOL. *Prospect, 14*(3), 32–39.

Weigle, S. C. (2014). Considerations for second language writing. In M. Celce-Murcia, M. A. Snow, & D. Brinton (Eds.), *Teaching English as a second or foreign language* (4th ed., pp. 222–237). Boston, MA: National Geographic/Cengage Learning.

Wendler Shah, R. (2015). "It was sort of hard to understand them at times": Community perspectives on ELL students in service-learning partnerships. In J. M. Perren & A. J. Wurr (Eds.), *Learning the language of global citizenship: Strengthening service-learning in TESOL* (pp. 169–193). Champaign, IL: Common Ground.

Wurr, A. (1999). A pilot study of the impact of service-learning in college composition on native and non-native speakers of English. *Academic Exchange Quarterly, 3*(4), 54–61.

Wurr, A. J. (2001). The impact and effects of service-learning on native and non-native English speaking college composition students. Unpublished Doctoral diss., University of Arizona, Tucson.

Wurr, A. J. (2002). Service-learning and student writing: An investigation of effects. In A. Furco & S. Billig (Eds.), *Service-learning through a multidisciplinary lens: Advances in service-learning research, (Volume 2)* (pp. 103–121). Berkeley, CA: Information Age.

Wurr, A. J. (2009). Composing cultural diversity and civic literacy: English language learners as service providers. *Reflections: A Journal on Writing, Service-Learning, and Community Literacy, 9*(1), 162–190.

Wurr, A. J. (2013). Editorial. *TESOL Journal, 4*(3), 397–401.

Wurr, A. J., & Hellebrandt, J. (Eds.). (2007). *Learning the language of global citizenship: Service-learning in applied linguistics.* Bolton, MA: Anker/Wiley.

Wurr, A. J., & Perren, J. M. (2015). Introduction. In J. M. Perren, & A. J. Wurr, *Learning the language of global citizenship: Strengthening service-learning in TESOL* (pp. 1–24). Champaign, IL: Common Grounds Publishing.

Yeh, C. J., & Inose, M. (2003). International students' reported English fluency, social support satisfaction, and social connectedness as predictors of acculturative stress. *Counselling Psychology Quarterly, 16*(1), 15–28.

Zeldenrust, G. (2017). Teaching pragmatics to newcomers to Canada. Unpublished MA thesis, Brock University, St. Catharines, Ontario.

Zlotkowski, E. (1998). A new model of excellence. In E. Zlotkowski (Ed.), *Successful service-learning programs. New models of excellence in higher education* (pp. 1–14). Bolton, MA: Anker.